SPIRITUAL LIFE
2131 LINCOLN ROAD, N.E.
WASHINGTON, D.C. 20002

YIELDING TO COURAGE

Also by Judith C. Lechman

The World of Emily Howland
The Spirituality of Gentleness

YIELDING TO COURAGE

The Spiritual Path to Overcoming Fear

Judith C. Lechman

1817

Harper & Row, Publishers, San Francisco

Cambridge, Hagerstown, New York, Philadelphia, Washington
London, Mexico City, São Paulo, Singapore, Sydney

152.4
Le Y

FIRST EDITION

Library of Congress Cataloging-in-Publication Data

Lechman, Judith C.
  Yielding to courage.

  Bibliography: p.
  Includes index.
  1. Spiritual life. 2. Fear—Religious aspects—Christianity.
I. Title.
BV4501.2.L422 1988   241'.4   87-46215
ISBN 0-06-065222-5

---

88 89 90 91 92 RRD 10 9 8 7 6 5 4 3 2 1

To Tony
age-old son, newfound friend,
and growing yielder to courage

and

In memory of Deanna and Kay
whose brief journeys expressed
the courage of love

Contents

Acknowledgments

This book could not have come into being without the loving courage and support of my husband, Bern Lechman. I am also grateful for the encouragement of those family members, friends, and companions who gave unstintingly of their time, resources, and skills to help improve this work. In particular, I am indebted to Priscilla Brown, Jim Lenhart, Betti Colucci, Frank and Mary Ann Lechman, Anthony and Winifred Bond Colucci, and Gail Roberson for their considerable contributions. I also thank Christine M. Anderson at Harper & Row for her invaluable and cheerful assistance in preparing this manuscript. Finally, I wish to express my deepest appreciation to my editor, Roy M. Carlisle, for his unfailing sensitivity and faithfulness to the process of creating this book.

Introduction: The Call

We live in a fearful age. We fear others, and we fear God. We fear the nameless dread that awakens us from sleep in the middle of the night, and we fear the named dread of nuclear holocaust that invades our waking thoughts and dreams. Most significantly, we fear our spiritual journey through this life, a journey that leads us ever closer to God and self.

When we begin this inner journey of growth, we don't see that the pathway ahead of us winds through landscape unique to each individual. Nor can we see that in moving toward God, we also gain a deeper knowledge of self. Ironically, only when we choose to center our lives on the Holy do we discover the necessity of making our selves whole. Thus, we embark on the most difficult of journeys, made nearly impossible by the fact that we must confront the full evilness of fear as we travel.

Initially, the fear that we encounter is relatively benign. We are afraid of the changes about to take place in our lives. The unknown and unknowing scare us into stopping and taking stock of where we're headed and why. We realize that we're reacting naturally to the very real risks and suffering that change will bring, and we are reassured by this awareness.

Later in our journey, though, the source of our fear becomes less obvious and more insidious. It dons different guises to match the stages we enter. Sometimes fear appears dressed as despair. At other times, it wears the mask of impotent rage. Occasionally we may even see it cloaked in our acts of selfishness or in our divisive words.

Fear no longer is a natural response to change. Rooted in evil, it has become the single, most important obstacle that we must overcome on the pathway to spiritual maturity. Fear, unrecognized or ignored, separates us from God, ourselves, and others. Fear, unchecked or underestimated, cripples, paralyzes, and, ultimately, destroys our relationships and our spirits.

Fear rooted in evil holds a terrible power over us. Yet this need not be so. We don't have to succumb to the tyranny of fear as we travel to God at the center. We can search for fear's evil roots and expose them. Tearing off the myriad masks of fear, we can name them. As we strip away the different disguises, we are able to confront fear directly.

Unfortunately, exposing, naming, and confronting fear isn't enough to destroy its power in our lives. To do that, we must replace fear with the courage demanded in the nearly five hundred Old and New Testament calls to be not afraid, to fear no evil, and to experience fearlessness. In those biblical calls to courage, we are asked to accept four specific challenges that together bring us from a fearful state to a courageous one. To grow, to mature, to approach wholeness and a vision of God, we have no choice but to accept the challenges to move (1) from *despair* to *confidence,* (2) from *weakness* to *strength,* (3) from *selfishness* to *caring,* and (4) from *divisiveness* to *harmony.*

In each challenge, we recognize that we need to face a particularly evil aspect of fear and move through it and beyond to a new reality in which we live lives of authentic and effective courage. Each challenge is a miniature journey reflecting the larger one of which it is a part. We begin each journey in the darkness of evil and stumble along through confusion, doubt, dryness, and isolation. Inextricably, we become caught in a maelstrom of despair, alienation, loss, and suffering, before we are bathed in the healing light of a more perfect love, companionship, and harmony.

These four challenges can be systematized no further. They make their appearance in our spiritual lives in no particular order. The only thing we know for certain is that we shall face them again and again on ever deepening and demanding levels.

Our lives are in constant movement between fear and courage, ebbing and flowing between the poles of meaninglessness and assurance, powerlessness and gentle might, isolation and compassion, and conflict and peace. The more we understand the evil that underlies our fear, the freer we will be to move toward the cornerstones of courage.

With that freedom come additional responsibilities and demands. The focus changes from self to God and others. In coming to terms with the reality of evil within us, we find that we must deal with the evil that exists in the world around us. As we reduce the power of fear in our lives, we in turn learn to accept the awful vulnerability that comes with our growing mastery of courage. Now open to the problems of others, we feel the agony and pain of our fellow humans on their life journeys.

There is no other route we can take to reach courage. Yet, if it is an odyssey filled with hurt, it is also one of great happiness. We discover the quiet joy of learning, of exercising our faith, of disciplining our minds and emotions. We also delight in our growing intimacy and communion with God. The mysterious blessings of grace gladden our hearts, making the lonely and difficult moments more bearable.

In accepting the four challenges, we are following a map that points us toward the final goal of each spiritual journey: to live a life of good courage unceasingly in the presence of God. Rejecting our separation through fear from the divine, we search for ways to meet forthrightly and overcome the evil present in our own lives and in the lives of those around us. Daring to be transformed into courageous followers of Christ, we strive for healing and wholeness in this world as well as for salvation in the world to come.

This is the pathway to courage and to God. Through the pages of this book, let us walk it together.

I. THE FIRST CHALLENGE
Moving from Despair to Confidence

The Lord is my light and my salvation;
whom shall I fear?

(PS. 27:1)

1. Meaninglessness

Heart pounding, drenched in cold sweat, I sat up, gasping for breath, in the bed of the strange motel room. Reaching over, I turned on the bedside lamp and then sank back against the pillows. In the soft light that also helped dispel the darkness of my dream, I looked on the relaxed, unguarded face of my husband, peaceful in sleep. For him, there were no abrupt, panic-filled awakenings from a too-quickly forgotten dream. His anxious moments, no less difficult or severe than mine, came in the harsh light of full consciousness.

Slipping quietly out of bed and into the coolness of the night air on the balcony beyond the room, I fought a silent battle for control of my shaking body and equally shaken mind. Repeating a familiar litany, I acknowledged once again all the obvious reasons for this anxiety attack: our third and most traumatic move in eight months, the death of one of my closest friends, the physical distance from loved ones, and emotional distance from one of my sons.

In the pale moonlight of an autumn North Carolina night, I finally admitted that I was afraid. Fear held me tightly in its grip: gut-wrenching, spirit-devouring, body-destroying fear. And I understood its source at last.

For the first time in my life, I realized what intricately complex creations we human beings are. More than gene-reproducing mechanisms, more than mere physical organisms with amazing programming capacities, more than self-actualizing consciousness, we are finely balanced integrations of body and spirit. We exist in a realm that extends beyond the purely materialistic. Like the world we inhabit, we are spirit and matter, spiritual and physical. God-created, we reflect the interaction of these two realities, and ideally they stand united.

Body and soul, *soma* and spirit, do influence one another. For each of us, our physical health or illness is directly related to our spiritual well-being or dysfunction. For good or for bad, we become not only what we eat, but also what we dare to conceive, imagine, dream, and believe about ourselves, our role in the cosmos, and our relationship with the Divine.

Implicitly or explicitly, each of us holds a world view. We each have our own particular set of ideas and beliefs as to the essential nature of the universe and our place within it. Our individual visions are as narrow or as wide, as superficial or as deep, as our desire to grow.

Standing on that motel balcony, I felt, in the exhausted state of my body and spirit, the complex interaction between the two realms. I knew that the stress factors and major life changes that I had experienced the past year had hurt my health and shaken my view of the world. The threatening and unfamiliar had been testing and challenging all that I once held precious. I wasn't sure what I believed any more. I questioned my relationship with God, and I questioned the nature of this imperfect world. More to the point, I questioned the motives and actions of my Creator.

Why had God allowed my dearest friend to suffer so? For what godly purpose had I been violently uprooted—not once but thrice—in such a short span of time? What divine plan demanded that I be stripped of financial security, of the warmth of community, of the strength and support of fellowship, of the love of a family member, of the comfort of a home?

These questions were borne of a reality filled with loss and change. They soon led me into darker regions. If God were a redemptive and loving Being of goodness, I asked, then why was there suffering and evil? Why should I continue to nurture a world view paradoxically centered on a Divine Lover who allows a corrupt world to be filled with broken and fractured people? Why should I seek the numinous when doubts of the Holy seemed more real than the Presence Itself?

The moment of self-knowledge on the motel balcony, when I

recognized the source of my fear, was more shattering than the anxiety attack that led up to it. I discovered that both body and soul, *soma* and spirit, had become imbued with the very real evil of hopelessness. While questioning the nature of God, I had succumbed to evil in one of its purest forms. Moving beyond doubt, I had embraced meaninglessness.

Meaninglessness

We've all heard the phrase "when life has lost all meaning." Sometimes it rolls glibly off the speaker's tongue to fall among other clichés about hopelessness and despair. At other times, we hear the phrase intoned with a pompous solemnity and judgmental shake of the head. Occasionally, it is spoken with sensitivity and compassion. In the main though, we keep our distance from the basic *angst* of meaninglessness. Preferring to ignore the question of meaning in our lives, we find it easier to run from the issue than to confront it. Let me explain.

In leading workshops, giving speeches, and writing in the field of spiritual growth during the last decade, I've noticed a distinct, and not altogether surprising pattern emerge. Over the years, men and women approaching the middle of life have shared with me the pain they've felt from the lack of meaning in their lives. Rarely are they inactive people, uninvolved in their careers, loving relationships, or community affairs. Expending a great deal of energy, they tend to immerse themselves in one project after another. In their bustling to and fro, they vainly seek confirmation that their thoughts and actions have purpose and value.

Yet the very fear of meaninglessness that thrusts them into such frantic activity also makes them incapable of experiencing the Ultimate Validity, God. Feeling the glaring absence of all things divine, they begin to harbor a world view in which God and the realm of the spirit are seen as lies. Nothing spiritual exists. Only the physical, the materialistic, the observable are real. Life begins with birth and ends with death. Their hope that it may hold more meaning has turned into a despairing nothingness.

Spiritual beliefs have died, and faith in God is gone. Their pain knows no bounds. In story after story that they have told me, such loss rarely happened in a single moment. It occurred gradually as these people unknowingly stopped along the pathway of spiritual growth.

Our journey, like theirs, begins in questioning. We know so little about the spiritual and the physical realms. Having few answers and even less understanding about the cosmos or self, we seek knowledge of the universe, of the human body and mind, and of the divine. Admitting to our ignorance, we embark on a voyage of inner and outer exploration. As we leave behind the comfortable, familiar, and secure, we risk the unknown in hopes of understanding who we are and what our world was, is, and may become.

Our safe vision of reality has vanished. A new vision, based on expanded self-knowledge and a deeper communion with the Holy, is beyond our awareness. At this point, we are most tempted to turn away from the demanding task of learning and to embrace, instead, the nihilistic belief that our traditional values are unfounded and our existence both useless and senseless.

To succumb to this viewpoint is to sink into a place of evil dominated by the fear that creation truly is a cosmic joke. We become drifters, living life selfishly and cynically, for we have no meaningful destination in sight. Most distressing, we lose the capacity to feel joy. We view life as a series of steady losses, beginning with the loss of innocence, progressing to a loss of faith, and ending with the loss of life in the finality of death.

I came face to face with this evil during my first year of work-study as a psychiatric social worker during the early 1960s. Assigned to the women's back ward of a state mental institution outside Bangor, Maine, I saw—for the first time in my sheltered existence—the ravages of illness on the human body, mind, and spirit.

Writing this twenty-five years later, I can still smell the sickening odor of unwashed bodies, feces, dried food, and urine. I imagine once more the pale sunlight falling through barred windows on the drooling, agitated, vacant, or violent faces of the patients. I find myself shivering, remembering again the coldly efficient click of the lock when the orderly left this dismal room, euphemistically called the Chronic Untidy Ward.

There I found so much suffering and so little meaning. My immediate supervisor made it abundantly clear that these women were unsalvageable, beyond rehabilitation or redemption. No progress was expected; therefore, no progress was made. I soon wondered how I ever thought I could create positive change or growth in even one life.

In a locked ward in the backwoods of Maine, I grew angry with God for allowing such pain to exist in this world. Later, my anger cooled into a hardened lump of despair. I considered spiritual growth toward God and wholeness a heartbreaking myth. This room with all its hopelessness was the only true reality, a reality chilling in its meaninglessness.

Fortunately, a wise and compassionate campus priest helped me to understand that meaninglessness is an evil roadblock on our journey through life because it is there that the darkness of the spirit meets the darkness of the physical. Without meaning in our lives, we can't function healthily in body or in spirit. In denying the spiritual, we bring our search for wholeness and God to an abrupt halt.

Even more devastating, this darkness within can extend beyond, touching those we meet in the course of the day. Our despair is a contagious sickness of the spirit every bit as life-threatening as a communicable physical disease. It infects the spirit of others, drawing them into the fear that is devouring us.

That is the nature of evil, and its power cannot be overstated. It influences our perceptions of the past, our dealings in the present, and our course of action for the future. When we are afraid, we look at the past and find no validity, we look at the present and find no meaning, and we look at the future and find no hope. This threefold aspect of meaninglessness festers at the very core of our despair.

The Past

To find meaning to our existence, we turn to the past. During this arduous and frustrating search, our growing awareness reflects our own imperfection. We soon realize that our knowledge is fragmentary and our understanding even more limited.

Driven to uncover answers about our world, ourselves, and the nature of God, we wield either the tools of science or those of religion. We choose skepticism or blind faith, testing or superstition, rigorous standards of evidence or received truth, hypotheses or revelation, proofs or unquestioned assumptions. Although these two approaches differ radically, we make our choices believing they will help release us from the shackles of ignorance and give life meaning.

Unfortunately, each new generation of seekers must learn anew that a solely intellectual, scientific world view will yield no more spiritual truth about the past than an equally dogmatic, religious one. Both are human approaches to enlightenment—limited, fragmentary, and imperfect.

By looking at the past with either a rigidly religious or scientific eye, we will never be able to bring God into proper focus. With a religious world view, we narrow our field of vision. In Christianity, for example, we traditionally define God as Father, as white-male-patriarch-on-a-throne-in-the-sky-bye-and-bye. We insist on fashioning "him" in the image of the dominant race and sex. Meanwhile we ignore the very real inconsistencies and contradictions present in reading "his" Word. Sadly, Christianity isn't alone in making these culture-bound claims and calling them spiritual truth. The sheer number of conflicting creeds defining the one true belief in the divine staggers the thoughtful seeker.

We can become equally disconcerted when we accept a scientific world view. Although our field of vision widens, we encounter a different set of difficulties. Now we see, with utter clarity, what has been done in the past in the name of God. Without the protective veil of religious dogmatism, we learn how we have violated the most basic standards of decency, compassion, and caring in following the tenets of a professed religion. We discover a history of human and animal sacrifices, of wars of persecution, of genocide, of the deliberate perpetuation of ignorance, slavery, racism, and sexism, of the steady escalation of cruelty, violence, and barbarism.

Looking back over recorded history, we learn that we have burned, maimed, pillaged, raped, tortured, and killed in appalling numbers for the alleged glory of God. Religious dogmatism has loosed on this world wholesale starvation, economic and social inequality, insanity, and countless other illnesses of the body and spirit. To the scientific mind, religion has impeded rather than helped make this earth a healthy, compassionate, safe, and loving place for humans to exist.

Even more upsetting, when we apply the scientific method to the Scriptures we find that such reprehensible behavior often wears the Almighty's seal of approval. We can't neatly assign these lapses to the avenging, retributive consciousness of the Old Testament God alone; that still leaves much to explain away in the New Testament, beginning with the slaughter of the innocent babes of Bethlehem and concluding with the bloody visions of the Apocalypse.

As we expand our knowledge, we discover, to our horror, that the God of love can and does speak in a contradictory, inconsistent, unsatisfactory, and unloving manner. Now we have moved beyond the safety net of blind faith. The knowledge we sought hasn't led us to enlightenment but rather to the darkness of doubt. No longer can we believe in the God of our childhood, the God of our parents, or the God of our former self. Having shed other people's concepts of God, we have no experience of our own reality of God to replace this loss.

We feel alone, abandoned, and deceived. Growth and change have brought us a deep and abiding sense of loss. The past holds no answers except the darkness that leads to despair. And when we look at the present for solace, we find it even less comforting.

The Present

A review of current events is a frightening catalogue of humanity's ills. Nuclearism, apartheid, international terrorism, gasoline-soaked tire "necklacing," environmental pollution, sexism in the workplace, guerrilla warfare, and the unequal distribution of resources, goods, and services are global and personal themes we hear sounded again and again.

Other public as well as private difficulties touch our lives more directly. We feel the strain of becoming a morally bankrupt society, and that strain is reflected in the statistics measuring our rising drug and alcohol abuse, suicides, abortions, teen pregnancies, illiteracy, the feminization of poverty, divorce, and racial and class polarization.

Turning on the television for education or escape, we see both the violent reality of everyday U.S. life and the equally destructive visions offered by televangelists preaching the gospel of material abundance. Discourses on genetic engineering compete with electronic faith healing. Visions of extravagant Christian resorts vie with images of starvation half a world away. Offensive religious principles for financial and emotional gain rival obscene secular schemes to "get rich quick" and "stay healthy and happy."

We are preached at to consume, to look out for ourselves as individuals and as a nation, to hate a godless political ideology, and to legislate a distorted Judeo-Christian morality into our political structure. Fed lies, we are told to call the process "sharing disinformation." Fed lies, we are also told, when politically expedient, to consider it "sharing the truth." We covertly sponsor murder in a sovereign country near our southwestern border and overtly fantasize about extending weapon systems into space. Although we have enough nuclear capability to destroy this planet and all life on it several times over, we steadfastly reject plans for significant disarmament.

We hear few sane voices, either secular or religious, in this wilderness of irrational sounds and frightful images. Caught in an intricate web of personal alienation, we discover the depth of our broken relationships with others, self, and God. Separated from the human and divine, we know the loneliness that accompanies despair. Our present lives hold less and less meaning as we grow more and more distant from wholeness. We feel the basis of our hope disappearing and are helpless to stop it.

The Future

When our thoughts turn to the future, our fear that life holds no meaning becomes readily apparent. No longer doubting our capacity for evil, we recognize that we have the wherewithal to commit nuclear genocide. At the very least, we can continue destroying the lands and seas of this planet while becoming a more violent and corrupt society.

On the most basic level, we admit to knowing nothing about the future except the certainty of our own deaths. Both the religious and scientific communities respond inadequately to this inevitable loss of life. The best they can give us is emotional and intellectual solace while exchanging conflicting opinions about the mysteries of life, death, and our evolution as a species.

A sense of hopelessness undergirds every fear-ridden scenario for the future. Failing to heal our fractured lives, science and religion alike convey dismal messages about our obvious powerlessness to cope with the loss and change ahead. While technological advances threaten our very existence, the Church offers few constructive alternatives to these threats.

The Necessity of Despair

When we reach this point in our thinking, we encounter the total darkness of our despair. Immersed in this frightful place, we feel we can travel no further on our journey. In searching to know the Creator and created better, we have come perilously close to losing our faith in both. We can fearlessly cry, "God is dead," but we can't add the essential, courageous refrain "Long live God!"

Until we realize that despair is an obstacle and not the final destination of spiritual growth, we will remain trapped in this spot, convinced that despair is where all questioning leads and ends. We need to learn that *within* our despair lies a liberating understanding of evil, and *through* our despair lies a liberating awareness of God.

Despair is a necessary step in our struggle to know God. And in meeting despair courageously, we meet, at last, the Deity whom we seek. This meeting will happen when we move beyond the religious and the scientific to experience a genuinely spiritual reality, in which we are able to come to terms with evil as well as with good.

As I write this last sentence, the memory of a magical autumn afternoon comes unbidden to my mind. Several years ago, I went to a clockmaker's shop set in the rabbit warren of back streets and alleyways of Old Town, Albuquerque, to interview the elderly owner. I can't recall now the thrust of the article I was writing. But I do remember clearly the unexpected and wide-ranging conversation we shared throughout that peaceful, golden afternoon.

Here was a man who loved his work. While we talked, I couldn't help noticing the way he would absentmindedly caress the wood of an antique mantel clock or lovingly polish an already spotless brass wheel. Surrounded by the gentle whispers of over two hundred ticking clocks, he explained why he knew neither loneliness nor despair. "In the sound of a clock I hear the voice of God," he said.

We, too, can hear God's voice in the commonplace sounds of our work. By experiencing the Divine Presence personally, we can let God give sacred meaning to every aspect of our lives. But to enter into this new spiritual reality, we first must learn how to open ourselves to the hope that exists within us and the world. Paradoxically, in the darkness as well as in the light, the means to master our fear and gain the confidence of courage can be found.

2. Hope

During my final days of living in New Mexico, I wanted nothing more than to slip away from the chaotic schedule of packing and saying goodbye to friends long enough to go into the desert. The closer the time came for me to leave my mountain home, the stronger the urge grew to spend a few precious hours in that desert spot I consider sacred.

The moment arrived when I could deny the inner prompting no longer. In the gray light of an early March morning, I drove down off the mountain and headed toward the familiar, barren expanse of the intermountain region I had grown to love so deeply. As I progressed, the waist-high snow by the roadside shrank to knee height and then became only ankle-deep before disappearing altogether.

Even without snow, the high country desert in late winter is a formidable place to be alone. The suffocating heat of summer has been exchanged for a biting cold that sears the lungs with every breath. The arroyos carved by flash floods after violent spring rainstorms are still forbiddingly difficult to cross almost a year later, while the decay written across the face of the autumn desert sends a gentler message than the deathly emptiness encountered now at winter's close.

Leaving the blacktop, my car bounced across the frozen ruts until the road came to a narrow end. Throwing on my knapsack filled with the essentials for desert hiking, I did what I had done countless times before: I entered the nothingness.

There is no other way to describe walking away from all the sensory input we receive in late-twentieth-century America. When I shut off the car engine, the tape of Vivaldi's *Four Seasons* came to an abrupt stop, too. Not even the soft crunching of my boots in the sand could diminish the overpowering silence that followed. Raising my eyes to the horizon, I saw there was nothing to interrupt my gaze. No houses, no trees, not even a hint of a mesa or butte. Nothing human-made nor God-created rose from this desert floor. And, as had happened each time I approached this land stripped of the familiar and comforting, I grew afraid.

That fear began with my awareness of being alone, separated from other humans in a space whose vastness defies simple measure. No signs of human life existed here; only I existed, standing alone in this place of rock and sandstone, scrub brush and cacti. Yet such knowledge didn't fill me with pride or self-importance. Instead, I felt quite the opposite. I was terrified. In the empty vast stillness of the desert, I had to confront the truth of my insignificance or run back to the safety of my car, my home, other people, and the busyness of life. In the desert, I had to accept that another reality exists beyond the world I have known, a reality in which I must come to terms with my living, my mortality, my aloneness, my dying. In the desert, all else is stripped away except these core questions of my existence.

No small wonder those ancient religions that arose in the deserts of the world referred to the desert wilderness variously as God's mind, heart, navel, and center. Even less wonder that all three of the world's monotheistic religions initially took root in the hearts of the desert people of the Negev and Sinai. In that desert, more than in the desert of the U.S. Southwest, a fearsome combination of emptiness and harshness is present. There, the vegetation is sparser, the mountains bleaker, the rock and sand more extensive, the heat more intense. While the gentler U.S. desert subtly attracts even the timid wanderer, the Negev and Sinai repel all but the most foolish and courageous. That stark stretch of desert in New Mexico is but a pale imitation of the gaunt holy peaks and wind-sculpted sand rifts of the desert that cradled Judaism, Christianity, and Islam.

Yet men and women of different centuries and cultures have encountered the same thing when exploring any of the deserts on the face of this earth. After the initial overpowering realization of a harsh and empty vastness comes fear. We all experience a deep abiding fear borne of an environment where all buffers between humans and nature, humans and humans, and humans and God have disappeared. We cannot find our bearings, for no bearings exist here. We are forced to recognize our smallness and to acknowledge how easily lost we can become, never to be found. We know that we are alone in this immense open space. Cut off from others, isolated from anything hospitable, we are left with only our selves, which we neither know nor understand.

The desert, then, becomes a place where we run headlong into that fear we most often avoid and refuse to name, a fear more elemental than that of our physical death. In the still desert void, we finally face and name our ageless human fear that life, all life, may have no meaning.

For me, the emptiness of the desert reflects the emptiness in our souls; the isolation of the desert mirrors the estrangement within our spirits. In the crowded moments of everyday life, I know I need not confront the emptiness or isolation I may feel. I can bury my fear that life holds no meaning with my busy schedule and smother it with other people and things. In the confines of my church and workplace and home, I don't have to explore the desert of self or come to terms with the basic fear underlying my very existence. But in the physical desert I'm not granted that safety or comfort. There, I must face a reality stripped of illusion, a reality that is the essence of spirituality.

In the desert, I feel that we have little choice but to discover that we no longer can rely on ourselves. Admitting our insignificance, we must look beyond and call to God with a hope arising out of utter desperation. Deep within our hearts, we realize that we have nowhere else to turn. We must search for God because without that seeking, our lives become truly meaningless. In such stillness, our souls cannot remain silent. We must confront our fear, grapple with it, grow with it, or we will die. We must cry out to a God, our God, in spite of our fear that in the void no Answer may exist.

In expressing our basic need for God, we meet head on the first paradox of the desert within and beyond: We search for the One we have already found. With our cry, we acknowledge the existence of God and our desire for a relationship with the Almighty. Our vision has expanded beyond the physical, dogmatic, or the self, beyond a scientific or religious reality or the fear-filled, self-centered one we imagine without God's presence. Out of the stillness of our fear and the void of the desert, we meet the Creator who has always been present. We hear what we could not hear before and see what has always been there.

We enter a new reality, a spiritual dimension that transcends our old limited concepts of time and sense and space. In reaching out to the One who has created all dimensions of reality, we feel a genuine response in turn. With a momentary flash of illumination, we know for certain that the God we have named and called out to and sought is real. The Almighty exists and is present within us and the world.

This awareness of God lasts but a moment, yet a moment is long enough. We have experienced God, and our wonder is boundless. For the first time, the joyous song of the psalmist touches our souls, affirming what we have just learned:

> The heavens declare the glory of God;
>> the skies proclaim the work of his hands.
> Day after day they pour forth speech;
>> night after night they display knowledge.
> There is no speech or language where their voice
>> is not heard.
> Their voice goes out into all the earth,
>> their words to the ends of the world.
>
> (PS. 19:1–4)

Yet more has occurred than discovering marks of the divine in nature and celebrating God as the Creator. In that brief moment when we cried out and were touched by God, a revolutionary relationship grounded in both belief and celebration began. Our selves, our lives, our world and cosmos gained meaning. From nothingness and despair—that desert of the self—came hope for a new life. Struggling to be heard by the God whose existence we had doubted, we found, instead, the fulfillment of this promise: "Fear not, for I have redeemed you; I have summoned you by name; you are mine. . . . For I am the Lord, your God" (Isa. 43:1, 3).

Something happened *within* us that corresponded with something happening *to* us. Only as we faced and named our fear did we hear the Supreme Being calling us. Moving beyond the fear-prescribed borders of our ordinary world, stripped of everything but the desire to encounter God, we found the Creator already waiting within our hearts.

Awakening to the Spirit

The first step taken from the fear of meaninglessness to the confidence of courage is our awakening to the Spirit within and beyond. As we grasp the reality of God's existence, we feel the hope in which confidence is born. We dare to believe that God will be with us as we experience life. The world remains uncertain and the future unknown, but now we have felt the presence of the Creator, and our focus has shifted. We have learned no more *about* God, yet we have begun to *know* God in that wondrous moment of awakening. Now we long for our knowledge to deepen and extend throughout all the moments of our lives. We are daring to enter a spiritual reality in which we seek to begin a relationship with the Infinite Being, to live life grounded in the Spirit, and to trust in the character and might of God.

In that fragile moment of spiritual awakening, we have touched and been touched by a Presence beyond our description and understanding. We sense that others have entered this reality, but we also know that our journey through it must be made alone. Our bond with the Deity is a deeply personal one. Although we only vaguely know who we are meeting, we realize we must approach God alone.

At this stage, I believe that we reach out to the Creator not so much to feel the reassuring power of the Almighty as to seek direction. Believing that God exists, we have entered into a relationship that is both a turning away from the evil of despair and a turning to the goodness of God, in which confidence is created. It is not coincidental that Christian conversion is grounded in this turning from fear and evil toward courage and goodness. The Old Testament word for the process of conversion, *shub*, means an actual turning around as we halt our movement in one direction and proceed in another, entirely different one. Similarly, two primary New Testament root words that refer to conversion, *metanoein* and *epistrephein*, stress the radical change of direction we take in faith after our spiritual awakening to the presence of God.

Over a thousand times in the Old Testament, we read that the people of the Sinai and Negev were called to move in a new direction away from their faithlessness to the one true living God, Yahweh. In the physical desert and the one within, these people of God, individually and corporately, were commanded to reverse the evil direction their lives had taken and to live new ones in full and utter faithfulness to God alone.

Turning in faith toward the Old Testament Yahweh marks the beginning, not the end, of humanity's awakening to the Spirit within and beyond. In the New Testament, we learn that the call to seek and know God in a deeply personal and faithful relationship has grown both more demanding and complex.

We first hear this call sounded by that holy man of the desert, John the Baptist. In his preaching, we discover the need for repentance, which is a turning away from a life of unfaithfulness. Next, we encounter the teachings of Jesus the Messiah and our need for salvation, which is a turning in faith to Christ as God incarnate, the Unknown made Known to us.

Responding to these calls to repentance and salvation, we recognize Jesus as the One who can restore us to that wholeness found in a life lived beyond fear. Only then do we experience and become filled with the empowering might of the Holy Spirit. The distant, yet always faithful God of the Old Testament has now revealed himself to us as the personal and loving God the Father *(Abba)*, God the Son (Jesus the Messiah), and God the Holy Spirit.

A New Relationship

Fragile in its newness, our relationship with the Triune God of the New Testament echoes the covenant of faith held by the people of Israel with Yahweh. Throughout the Word of God, we see the Deity as our deliverer. God is the One who hears our cries of despair and breaks the chains of fear that bind us before transforming our lives, our spirits, and our world. Time and again, we hear the Almighty say, "Do not fear; just believe" (Isa. 43:1,10; Mark 5:36).

In the Old Testament, we learn of the depth of Yahweh's loyalty to his people in story after story of his unwavering protection of them, his forgiveness of their sins, his delivering them from enemies and oppressors, and his continuing personal communion with them. In the New Testament, we discover that Jesus chose to live as a human being among us, to suffer as we do from the fears that arise from evil, to die a violent death, and to rise triumphantly so that we can be delivered from the power of evil. In Acts, we are taught about the gifts that grace the lives of those who hope, trust, and believe in Father, Son, and Holy Spirit. In the pages of the Bible, then, we are given countless lessons on divine faithfulness to those who seek to know God. We also learn how we must live our part of the relationship if we are truly to move beyond fear to the courage for which we were created.

To develop this relationship of faith with God is perhaps the most difficult move we will make on the spiritual journey from fear to courage. We can do nothing less than become open to God to the very core of self. Thomas Merton considered this stage in our development as "that deep change of heart in which we die on a certain level of our being in order to find ourselves alive and free on another, more spiritual level."[1]

This deep change of heart is a move from the kingdom of self to the kingdom of God, from the self-centered perspective of the humanist to the God-centered one of the holy. Our focus is firmly fixed on the Creator, not on the created. Having wandered in the emptiness of the desert within, we acknowledge that without God our existence is ultimately meaningless. When we placed God in the center of our lives, where the Divine Presence rightly belongs, our despair dissipates as the Spirit replaces self.

Here again, we encounter one of the many paradoxes we will meet while traveling in this spiritual reality. As we die to find ourselves alive and free, as we replace self with Spirit, we don't negate personality, character, or ego. Rather, we expand our awareness of who and what we are. Time and again, in the desert, I have come to know the nothingness of my spirit as I stand before and am touched by God. Returning to the world, I carry the Spirit within, which enriches every aspect of my life. In acknowledging my emptiness, I, at last, am filled. Now I am free to use my self—my knowledge, abilities, traits, strengths, talents, failings, interests, and weaknesses— to strive for Christlike wholeness in my work, my loves, my play, my sorrows.

Although our relationship with God begins in the desert, it cannot flourish there. We must bring it back into the world of people and places and events, the world in which Jesus of Nazareth lived, died, and rose again. Spiritual reality, through which we journey to courage, exists in the fullness of life, not in its absence. Present-oriented, it is rooted in the here and now as much as in the eternal. The central lesson of Jesus' teachings is that the good news of the kingdom of God in this world began with the Messiah's arrival. And the kingdom of

God is to be lived *in* this world and *of* the teachings Christ outlined in his Sermon on the Mount (Matt. 5–7; Luke 6).

According to New Testament scholar William Barclay, that Sermon "is nothing less than the concentrated memory of many hours of heart-to-heart communion between the disciples and their Master."[2] From that unique relationship, we have received a compendium of how to conduct all our relationships, human as well as divine. Given more than laws or regulations to govern our lives, we are shown a discernible lifestyle to emulate and a journey of growth to follow. We are taught what the kingdom of God on earth actually means:

- Realizing our own helplessness
- Mourning our sinfulness
- Putting our whole trust in God
- Placing ourselves into the complete control of God
- Striving wholly for goodness
- Caring wholly for others
- Desiring only God
- Being united with others doing God's work
- Singly and together fulfilling God's purpose no matter how painful.

The Sermon on the Mount moves us from establishing our relationship with God to living it out in the world of women and men today. It brings us from an awakening of the Spirit within to an ever-deepening awareness of self and how we choose to live in the kingdom of God. Being found by our Creator, we, in turn, find self-knowledge in this new reality. The emptiness, fear, and despair experienced in the spiritual desert of our lives is being replaced with a newfound understanding of both God and self. Surprisingly, the closer we draw to God, the greater our self-knowledge becomes. Saint Augustine's famous prayer, "May I know You, may I know myself," is as valid for Christians today as it was for this Church father sixteen centuries ago. But to know ourselves better so that we may know God better depends on our developing three crucial qualities: honesty, commitment, and wonder.

Honesty

Encountering God requires us to reach out to the Deity with an honesty that may be foreign to us and the way we've been relating to others in this world. We enter God's presence understanding that the One we seek is the God of truth. No deceit is permitted here.

The Christian writer C. S. Lewis, in his classic retelling of the myth of Psyche, recognized that very thing. In the conclusion of *Till We Have Faces*, he has the protagonist state, "I saw well why the gods do not speak to us openly, nor let us answer . . . why should they hear the babble that we think we mean? How can they meet us face to face till we have faces?"[3]

I have learned that I cannot present a mask to the Almighty. The face I dare to turn toward God needs to reflect the full truth existing within my mind, heart, and soul. No matter how good or evil that truth may be, I have little else to offer God except honesty. Knowing that lying removes me from God's presence, I speak the truth in order to close the distance existing between us. If I call out to the Lord in the honesty of my despair, I believe I'll receive an answer giving me hope anew that life has both meaning and purpose.

To explore the Source of this fledgling hope, I understand that we who make this journey must become ruthlessly honest with ourselves and the God we have begun to know. We no longer can keep parts of ourselves from God, much as we hide select portions of our lives and personalities from those we meet during the course of the day. We need to learn to trust God fully with who and what we are, for without this basic trust we will never be free from fear or be able to grow spiritually.

Learning this, it didn't surprise me to discover that "confidence" and "confide" stem from the same Latin root word *confidēre*, which means to abide with or trust. Courage, based on our growing confidence in God, cannot take hold in our spirits until we begin to confide in the Divine Spirit; that is, faithfully and honestly trust God with all we are at the present moment.

Commitment

To encounter God, we need to develop a second quality, one that takes us past the honesty of trusting God with our selves. Now we must commit our whole lives to the Almighty by exploring and following our vocations within this spiritual reality. Commitment becomes our unique response to what we are called to do and be once we enter the life of the spirit.

Having been touched by God, we now are summoned to holiness. Having sought God and been found, we must learn to heed the promptings of the Spirit and translate those promptings into practical, everyday action. When I reached this stage some years ago, I could barely conceive of the powers and grace bestowed on us by the Almighty. Yet I knew I had to ask myself how best to use the gifts of communication I had been granted as I continued on my spiritual journey. So it is for each of us. Our developing faith, hope, and trust in the Creator carry with them a profound commitment. We have been called to make our work and home lives, our friendships and community involvement, a reflection of all that is divine.

In learning honesty, we began to surrender ourselves to God with an open, often painful, awareness of all that we are. In learning commitment, we now surrender to God the moments of our lives. We bring to the Almighty not only all that we are but also all that we touch. We bring lives of action, lives of human relationships and events, lives of people, activities, and things.

In learning honesty, we submit to being known. In learning commitment, we submit to being used. But being used by God—following the vocation that fulfills God's purpose—is not a passive resignation to divine plans for our lives. Committing ourselves to God is a creatively active choice initiated by our Lord and completed by us.

A call whose summons we can either ignore or follow, our commitment is based on spiritual rather than worldly concerns. We realize that now we must search to find that work for which God has prepared us. And we are called to do it to the best of our abilities. Commitment makes our lives become something we live in union with God, not merely experience in a realm far removed from the holy. Unless we are committed to recognizing and listening to the workings of the Spirit in our lives, our relationship with God cannot grow.

Wonder

The final quality we need to establish our relationship with God appears deceptively simple: a sense of wonder. In our initial contact, we entered the presence of God with fear and trembling, and all too often, it was a fear and trembling over our own lostness rather than over the grandeur and might of God.

Our first experience of the Almighty uplifted us, but it wasn't transcending. Having submitted to being known and used by God, we now want to become infused with the Spirit that transforms us on the most elemental level of our beings. In her book *In Search of the Spirit*, Mary McDermott Shideler accurately described our desire as one where "We surrender to the ultimate, the invasion becomes an impregnation, and from the union of the finite person with the infinite ultimate is born a new life."[4]

Although this spiritual birth is a source of wonder, it's but a tiny reflection of the Source of all creation. Yet how casually we approach the Creator with our words and thoughts and actions that express neither the reverence nor the intimacy our relationship with God demands. We would do well to consider Saint Teresa of Avila's constant reminder to her young novices to ponder the majesty and the love of God as they tried to walk the Way of Perfection. Both she and her contemporary, Saint John of the Cross, looked on their relationship with God as a consummating experience with a Divine Lover, one "that joined Beloved with lover, lover transformed in the Beloved!"[5]

I have yet to experience such a degree of reverent intimacy, which leaves no room for the evil of despair. Instead, I have known brief moments infused with wonder. During them, I've felt the loving presence of a Creator with power over evil, a presence amazingly seeking deeper communion with me. Transformed by these experiences, I know I must continue to nurture the loving bonds that exist between God and myself.

I suspect that for each of us these bonds of love have the power to replace meaninglessness with divine purpose, fear with faith, and despairing evil with an unshakable confidence in the Almighty. When we are able to relate to God with this loving honesty, commitment, and wonder, we know we're ready to enter with confidence into a life of the spirit.

Our first steps as spiritual novitiates led us into the desert where we experienced fear and heard the divine call to courage. There, we discovered our belief in God's existence, trust in God's purpose for our lives, and an abiding hope grounded in God's loving, wondrous nature. Now, we approach the world of prayer, where we will learn the discipline needed to live the confidence of courage.

3. Assurance

When we live a life of prayer, we experience assurance, which is confidence in God and the courage to live that confidence wholly. Ironically, our journey toward assurance and prayer begins the moment we choose to consider life meaningless, to fear our own interior emptiness in a world devoid of divine purpose, and to succumb to the resulting feelings of despair.

Out of this despair, we take our initial steps toward prayer. Separated from the Creator, our spirits pained, we call out in the void caused by our fear to the only One who can heal this fracture. Overcome by the evil of despair, we don't expect to receive an answer. Yet, with the grace of the Almighty, we are gifted with the Divine Presence within and beyond.

We begin a tentative relationship with the Deity, based on a fragile spark of hope that flares more brightly as we learn to know the Deity incarnate, Jesus Christ. Although sinners, we experience a liberating salvation in his name. Through the power of the Holy Spirit, that spark soon becomes a steady flame of trust and reliance on this personal, loving, and redeeming God, a God whom we approach now with honesty, commitment, and a wondrous reverence.

We have entered a new reality, the spiritual domain, where transformation and change are necessary if our relationship with God is to flourish. The strands of our spiritual growth and our communion with the Spirit are inextricably woven together. We cannot attain wholeness without an authentic deepening of our union with God. A journey toward spiritual wholeness becomes a journey toward God. And that pathway we follow takes us from evil to goodness, from fear to courage, from hopelessness to trust, from despair to confidence, and from meaninglessness to assurance.

Transformation and change are the keys to our growth within the spiritual domain, and these occur through prayer. "To pray is to change," Richard Foster wrote in *Celebration of Discipline*. "Prayer is the central avenue God uses to transform us."[1]

We change, and we are transformed. In prayer, we actively seek to become more Christlike. We also passively ask the Lord to do with us what is divinely willed. Through prayer, we participate in becoming new people in Christ. We also accept the transformation that God alone can make in our spirits and our lives.

Prayer is the fulcrum on which our spiritual lives balance. Prayer, properly practiced, keeps us centered between the extremes of an active involvement, independent of obedience to God's will, and a passive resignation, independent of the sincere desire to do God's will. Prayer helps us maintain total dependence on the Creator while taking responsibility for the direction of our spiritual lives. We pray so that we may be directed toward those ends God has chosen for us. We also pray that we may grow in our awareness of God, our receptivity to God's purpose, and our capacity to obey and fulfill it.

I shouldn't have been surprised to discover that our individual prayers lead us inexorably toward the same vocation. No matter how different our circumstances, we all are called to submit our lives to the Almighty and to stop all resistance to the divine working within us. Although I realize that few of us harbor any intention of becoming hermits, our shared vocations are much the same as those of the desert mothers and fathers, those fourth-century holy women and men who chose to turn their backs on a corrupt society to live lives of prayer in the Sinai and Negev. Speaking for them, Abba Cassian stated that "the ultimate end of our profession is the kingdom of God . . . the proximate end, to which we direct our immediate strivings, is purity of heart."[2]

We soon learn that this search for sanctity and God's kingdom is fueled only through prayer, for there we meet Christ, who is master of the spiritual life and the way of prayer. The gospels record fourteen instances when Jesus prayed for purity of heart and for establishment of the kingdom of God. Studying them, we discover that Christ prayed in preparation for each of the major events in his ministry, in obedience to a will other than his own, in gratitude, in humble petition, in times of testing, and in times of thanksgiving. And when his disciples asked him to teach them to pray, he did so by word and by deed.

Jesus taught them that prayer is a constant communion between Creator and created: a petition in his name that will be answered by the Father, a promise made in faith to be divinely fulfilled, a relationship nurtured both in solitude and in the company of other believers, a source of power, an expression of commitment, a simple, yet extraordinary surrender. In the Scriptures, we discover that life in the spirit is a life of prayer. It includes all the moments, thoughts, desires, and concerns of our days, minds, bodies, and hearts.

In my discipleship group, we have developed a working definition of prayer, one that keeps expanding and being refined as we explore the depths of prayer together. We began with this definition:

Prayer is not just something we do at certain times of the day in our week between Sundays. It is a lifestyle of who we are in relationship with God based on an attitude of communication and fellowship with the Almighty.[3]

Several months later, we recognized the inadequacy of our words in describing this continual yearning of our spirits toward God, this pervasive Presence guiding our lives, this gentle Heart controlling ours. We're finding that there are as many facets to prayer as there are ways to communicate.

Prayer reflects both finite humanity and the infinity of the Almighty. In the beginning of our spiritual journey, we experiment with various forms, styles, and rituals in communicating with God. We learn different types of prayer for different occasions. We meditate in the silence alone or with others. We contemplate in solitude, sing psalms in public worship, and shout in praise and adoration. We whisper a hurried word of thanks, beg for forgiveness, cry for help, yearn for comfort, and weep for strength. Even as fledgling Christians, we instinctively seem to know that we must bring all parts of ourselves before God, that for some inexplicable reason, God wants to know us, the created, fully in a revelatory process based on trust and concern and love.

Praying becomes a way of revealing, bit by bit, who we are in relation to the One in whose image and likeness we have been made (Gen. 1:26, 27). Gradually, we learn that our fellowship with God and our journey toward that wholeness capable of healing our fear-filled spirits remains personal and individual, yet follows a pathway others have traveled.

If we are to grow in courage, we must use increasingly more of our imagination, resourcefulness, intelligence, and tenacity in unison with the Almighty. Although our walk with God is still uniquely our own, others can offer valuable help on this journey. They have searched for the way of prayer that leads us from the hope we have discovered in despair to the confidence of courage grounded in the reality of God. They have walked on the path of assurance and left signposts for us along the way. It is to these pilgrims we gratefully turn our attention now.

The Way of Assurance

The eloquent seventeenth-century French cleric and mystic François de Salignac de la Mothe Fénelon, understood that the way of assurance leads through prayer. In a thoughtful letter to one of the many people he counseled during his lifetime, Fénelon outlined this pathway appropriately enough in the form of a prayer:

I simply present myself before Thee. I open my heart to Thee. Behold my needs, which I know not myself; see and do according to Thy tender mercy. Smite, or heal; depress me, or raise me up; I adore all Thy purposes without knowing them; I am silent; I offer myself in sacrifice; I yield myself to Thee; I would have no other desire than to accomplish Thy will. Teach me to pray; pray Thyself in me.[4]

These devout words weren't written by one far removed from the tensions and problems of the world. This heartfelt prayer was penned by a man who had risen to one of the highest positions of political and religious authority in the France of Louis XIV. He was responsible for the education of the king's grandson, had received numerous awards, including membership in the French Academy of Letters, was Abbé of Saint Valery and Archbishop of Cambrai. He also had developed a deepening relationship with Jesus Christ under the guidance of the controversial Madame Guyon. When she came under attack for her teachings on the necessity of experiencing and expressing a selfless love for God and was imprisoned as a heretic, Fénelon admitted to the dangers of some of her teachings, yet bravely refused to denounce her as a criminal.

By aligning himself with Madame Guyon and against both civil and church powers, Fénelon quickly fell out of favor with Louis XIV and the Vatican, was banished to a remote diocese for the remainder of his life, had his writings denounced by the Roman Catholic Church, and wasn't permitted to visit even his closest friends. Instead of becoming a bitter and broken man, Fénelon used these difficult years in exile before his death to attend to the humble duties of running the diocese and to corresponding with those he had been banned from seeing.

Rather than being crushed by the isolation and disgrace that he suffered for his spiritual beliefs, the Archbishop devoted these final years to strengthening his communion with God. Living his faith, Fénelon exhibited an authentic courage that was based on an unshakable confidence in God. As his adversities mounted, his assurance in the loving, faithful, and personal nature of the Deity grew. His letters reflected this growth, giving increasingly wise counsel and direction to those who shared their spiritual problems and questions with him.

The prayer quoted earlier was one the Archbishop wrote to his friend, the Duke of Beauvilliers, in answer to a query on how to pray. In his response, Fénelon outlined the six steps we need to take to communicate with God:

1. "I simply present myself before Thee."
2. "I open my heart to Thee."
3. "I adore all Thy purposes without knowing them."
4. "I am silent."
5. "I offer myself in sacrifice."
6. "I yield myself to Thee."

These six steps are more than a means of relating to the Almighty. They indicate the way we must follow if our assurance is to grow. Prayer not only is a vehicle we use to communicate with God. It's also the means by which both our confidence in God and our courage to live lives centered in the Spirit increase. Learning how to pray becomes the way to assurance, and there are few wiser teachers along this particular pathway than the disgraced Archbishop of Cambrai, François Fénelon.

Taking the First Step: Be Still

It's revealing that Fénelon doesn't begin his prayer by asking for anything. He recognizes that God knows our strengths and failings, our needs and desires better than we do. Any words that we speak as we enter the presence of the Almighty are apt to be distracting. To stand before God, we need only present ourselves simply; that is, with a single-minded focus on God. No words are necessary when our full attention is centered on the divine.

In the beginning, we gain such concentration by quieting the activities of our busy daily lives. We consciously take time out to still our minds, bodies, and feelings, to think purposefully only of God, to concentrate quietly on our growing awareness and need for the Divine Presence within our hearts. We move away from the details of everyday life—the business appointment to keep, the family discussion we just had, the shopping to be done, the recent conversation with a close friend, the children to be chauffeured—in order to meet God. It seems that we must move away from all else to move closer to God.

It was at this stage that I entered the New Mexican desert last March. Sadly enough, the painful reality of leaving my home had overpowered the greater reality of God. I knew that I had to retreat to that place of nothingness and be still before I could feel the healing, nurturing, and loving Divine Presence once again.

For the spiritual novitiate, being simply present means the absence of thoughts, words, and activities that interfere with our focusing wholly on God. In time, more will be demanded from us. Prayer, true prayer grounded in a simple interior stillness before the Lord, demands that we become fully attentive to God in the midst of life, not when we remove ourselves from it. "This way of prayer is not a struggle to keep recollected *in spite of* work, travel, or other activities," Thomas Merton counsels us in *Contemplative Prayer,* "but flows from everyday life and is in accord with work and other duties."[5]

We now realize that prayer is rooted in life. Practicing the presence of God must take place in an interior stillness that touches all the moments of our lives. In this way we are led toward the second step on the pathway to knowing assurance in God and gaining the confidence of courage.

Taking the Next Step: Be Open

One of the great psalms of David cautions us not only to "be still before the Lord" but also to "wait patiently for him" (Ps. 37:7). Patient waiting requires an expectant openness, an ability to be alert to God's presence in our lives. With our concentration fixed firmly on God, we anticipate being touched by the divine in return, if we but remain ready.

When Fénelon wrote, "I open my heart to Thee," he was making a statement of discipline. It takes practice to remove all else from our hearts so that God may enter. We must repeatedly acknowledge the fears, the doubts, and the questions we have about our relationship with God, place them openly before the Lord, and together work to overcome them.

When I entered the desert that late winter day, I did so in expectation of encountering God. That expectancy, that readiness to be still and wait in the void for God's touch, meant that I was opening myself to experiencing my fear as well as my hope. In the desert, I had to face the overpowering fear that God might not respond, the doubt that I might not be led by the Spirit, and the despair that my life might not be God-directed. I couldn't be open before God until I had revealed my questions and fears and doubts. I also had to confess my hope and belief in the promise that God was already present, answering, leading, and determining every aspect of my life.

Rooted in the honesty we've begun to develop, openness requires us to become defenseless and remove the barriers behind which we hide so that we may be truthful with ourselves and with God. To seek the truth within and, at the same time, allow the Truth to seek us, we must be ready to count ourselves among the vulnerable. When God's Son lived among us, he chose to become one with the most vulnerable, a lesson we sometimes overlook when studying the Master's life. We can't work through the evil of despair or attain confidence in God until we dare to reveal our whole trembling selves to God.

This vulnerable openness is far easier to write about than to achieve. Thankfully, I have found it both something worked for and a gift divinely given. While seeking actively to become open, we gratefully discover the Holy Spirit helping us to bring everything that rests in our hearts before God. In this second step of prayer, as our barriers to vulnerability and openness are removed, we feel the chasm between the Creator and created closing. And for a brief moment, we are suspended in eternity, glimpsing the Unknown and feeling divine power and glory infuse our very souls.

Taking the Third Step: Be Adoring

Having been simultaneously awakened and infused at a depth where nothing but God can penetrate, we move from standing to kneeling before God. Bending our knees as a physical expression of our adoration, we acknowledge that our relationship with God is not one between equals. God is our Master, and, we, heeding the psalmist's advice, pay homage:

> Come, let us bow down in worship,
> let us kneel before the Lord our Maker;
> for he is our God
> and we are the people of his pasture,
> the flock under his care.
>
> (PS. 95:6–7)

The psalmist described his intimate and awe-filled relationship with God in terms of the Shepherd and his sheep, for God, to him, was a powerful yet loving Protector. How we choose to describe God reflects our own experiences on our spiritual journey. Whether we call God Spirit, King, Light, Mother, Father, Divine Artist, Deity, Almighty, Supreme Being, Deliverer, Savior, Redeemer, Refuge, or Infinite Being, we soon discover that words are limiting facets of the limitless. We'd do well to remember Martin Luther's biting comment to the famous humanist Desiderius Erasmus of Rotterdam, when he came to Luther's defense in his fight against the Roman Church: "Your thoughts of God are too human."[6] Like Erasmus, we need to stop defining our Creator in terms of human knowledge and to learn, instead, adoration for a nature beyond human boundaries.

In the first moments of genuine adoration, we discover that our experience of God cannot possibly be contained in a single image. Our fear of a meaningless existence, and the despair that arises from that fear, is replaced with a much different fear, one rooted in goodness rather than evil. In this third step of prayer, we find that to adore the Lord is to fear the Lord. "For the child of God, the primary meaning of the fear of God is veneration and honor, reverence and awe," Jerry Bridges wrote in *The Practice of Godliness*. "It focuses not upon the wrath of God but upon the majesty, holiness, and transcendant glory of God."[7]

Evil fear fills us with dread; the fear of God fills us with courage. Evil fear drains us of hope and confidence; godly fear infuses us with the assurance that destroys the basis of our despair. In prayer, we stand and are still before God. We learn to wait patiently with open hearts ready for that blessed moment of meeting and being met. In that holy encounter, we bow down in worship to the One whose nature is beyond our comprehension. Yet, no matter how incomplete our image of God may be, we kneel before our Creator deeply aware and adoring, for God does exist and we have glimpsed infinite might, love, and glory.

In my desert experience in New Mexico, I found that being still and open led to an overpowering, almost shattering, reality of God. I imagine that God touches each of us in a uniquely individual way. With me, the Divine Presence that winter day was as fearsome and mighty, wild and grand as the desert in which I had turned so often to seek God. That holy touch on my soul was more like a lightning bolt than a gentle glow, searing away the evil of despair and destroying all fear but that loving one of God.

Taking the Fourth Step: Be Silent

When François Fénelon prayed, "I am silent," he meant something quite different from the stillness we learned in the first step on the pathway of assurance. Although closely related, stillness and silence are separate practices that together enrich our communion with God. In becoming still, we took the responsibility of quieting our selves in preparation for our encounter with God. In becoming silent, we progress past this quieting. Already feeling God's presence and acknowledging divine sovereignty in our lives, we now become silent to hear God.

Silence is a listening act, one which we do with our hearts. But listening cannot begin until we have controlled the tongue, described by James as "a world of evil among the parts of the body. It corrupts the whole person" (James 3:6). Uncontrolled speaking leads us in one direction—toward sin. Just as the psalmist knew that adoration was a critical part of his communion with God, he also realized the necessity of silence in prayer: "I will watch my ways and keep my tongue from sin; I will put a muzzle on my mouth" (Ps. 39:1).

Yet, as a member of a society accustomed verbally to "letting it all hang out," I rarely heed the psalmist's advice. I am as guilty as the next of smothering my relationships with the spoken word and rushing to blanket with indiscriminate speech any pauses that may occur. In that rush, neither control nor listening becomes possible. Harboring the fear that silence holds a dreadful emptiness, I hurry to fill it with what too often is thoughtless conversation.

Once we have encountered God, though, we find silence to be a new means of experiencing the divine more deeply. In the silence of prayer, our despair over God's absence has been replaced with confidence in God's continuing presence. The empty silence that we feared has been converted into a full one in which we are capable of hearing God's voice and responding.

In the silence, God calls to us and, as Saint Teresa wrote with her usual directness, "hearing His voice is a greater trial than not hearing it."[8] This call to us is also a call asking us to invite others to join our journey. Listening to God's voice, we can hear the voices of our sisters and brothers and realize that we must reach out to both God and them. Learning silence, we are called to teach others as we are being instructed. Hearing what God wants of us, we are to share those instructions with others. In silence, we seek fuller understanding of God's will for us and our dependence on the Almighty. Out of that same silence, we are asked to lead others to a conscious awareness and dependence on God.

Before we communicated with God in the silence, we were tormented by the evil of despair and false visions of a meaningless existence. After hearing God, we face that greater trial about which Saint Teresa spoke. Responding to the Voice of hope and meaning with growing trust, we are asked to bring that message of hope and meaning to others beseiged by evil fear. In the silence, God has come into the center of our lives. Out of the silence, we are asked to bear witness to that centering.

Taking the Fifth Step: Be Sacrificing

The start of Jesus' public ministry began with his baptism by John at the Jordan. Unexpectedly, Jesus turned away from the noisy crowds of pilgrims at the river's edge and the anxious authorities closely monitoring the Baptizer's revolutionary message of repentance. Led by the Spirit, Christ turned to the desert, that harsh wasteland nearby known as the Wilderness of Zin. There, for forty days and nights, he fasted, after which, the Gospel of Matthew records with more than a touch of understatement, "he was hungry" (Matt. 4:2).

Until I had lived in the U.S. Southwest, I had never given much thought to the start of his ministry. Only as I reflected on it in the desert did I understand the significance of this event. Filled with the Holy Spirit after his baptism, Jesus willingly followed its leading, one that took him away from the world into a place and practice that would draw him ever close to his Father. Going without food and water for forty days and nights in the demanding environment of the

Wilderness of Zin also brought his human body to the point of starvation and death. Jesus' nearly six-week fast was no mere dietary inconvenience. It was a life-threatening offering of himself and a surrender of his body and spirit to God and his control. Jesus' fasting in the desert foreshadowed all the sacrifices of his three-year ministry, which culminated with his death on the cross. In the desert, Jesus centered his life on God, listened and heard God's will, and prepared himself to respond. He disciplined his body and his spirit to fulfill God's purpose, becoming a willing participant in the sacrifices required of him.

We, too, are called to be sacrificing, to offer ourselves willingly for God's purpose, no matter what the consequences. It isn't enough that we want to live lives of goodness. When we offer ourselves in sacrifice to God, our own desires and goals no longer are central. As Mary McDermott Shideler reminds us, "the virtuous person has committed himself to righteousness; the holy one has given himself to the ultimate."[9]

Following the way of assurance, we must give ourselves to God, always ready to come when we are called. We can't know in what ways we will be asked to submit our bodies and spirits to God. At different stages of our spiritual development, we will find the request from the Deity distinctly varied, yet the purpose forever remains the same. If we are to develop the confidence of courage, if our lives are to be an expression of our confidence in the holy character of the Almighty, we must be willing to emulate Jesus' sacrifice and surrender everything into the Father's control. On the spiritual path of assurance, we do more than kneel in awe at the feet of God. We place our lives in God's hands, knowing that, whatever the price, we choose to heed the divine call.

Taking the Final Step: Be Yielding

The last step in living this prayer of assurance is the most active response we make to the problem of evil and meaninglessness in our lives. Up to this point, our prayers have moved us *to* God and discerning the divine purpose for our lives. Now we allow ourselves to be moved *by* prayer to accomplish God's will. When we pray Fénelon's words, "I yield myself to Thee," we engage ourselves in the struggle to surrender on every level of our beings, making belief and action become one.

Yielding ourselves leads us out of the desert back into the world where we have been charged to establish the kingdom of God. In the desert, we sought and received that mysterious gift of the Spirit, which made us new women and men of God. This transformation took place within the person, but it is incomplete if we allow it to stop here. In yielding, we move beyond giving control to God. Now, we willingly allow God to make all things new in our lives, to transform the created, and to reestablish the world, through us, in Christ. Our prayers, which began in the stillness of the desert, grew in the expectant silence of our open and reverent hearts. They flourished through our offerings of sacrifice, empowering us to enter the world transformed and to transform the evil that exists there, too.

Our first five steps of prayer brought us increasingly closer to God. In the sixth step, in yielding, we work with God to establish the divine kingdom on earth. In imitation of the Son of God, we must leave the desert and go back into a world that is controlled, abused, and dominated by people who live in a reality other than the spiritual. But we are changed. We know our true identity. We belong to God. We are men and women of God, children of Light, Christians. We return to the world, but our allegiance is with God. We are of the spiritual realm, not the earthly one. We've entered life in the Spirit, and we are firmly grounded in the Eternal. Having heard the call to courage, we've responded by yielding ourselves to God. Transformed within, we have become God's agents of change in the world.

The Rhythm of Assurance

When I had my desert experience, I felt I had no choice but to follow this path of assurance. I was certain that my deep longing for the One, who alone makes existence meaningful, would be enough to conquer the particularly evil fear that God was absent in my life and the world. In my pain, I cried aloud the Teacher's universal lament when confidence in the Almighty ebbs: "Meaningless! Meaningless! Utterly meaningless! Everything is meaningless" (Ecc. 1:2). Yet, these words were no sooner spoken than I remembered the Teacher's final counsel to fear this Deity I longed for and loved. In awe, I listened in the silence and heard God's call before responding at a depth of surrender and yielding I previously would have considered impossible.

I had walked this pathway before and, at that moment, I knew I would be walking it again, for the way of assurance is one in which we learn and relearn the most basic lessons time and again. Less than nine months later, on the balcony of a motel in North Carolina in the middle of the night, I found myself retracing these six steps of prayer and relearning, once more, the lesson of *confidēre* in the Creator. Such movement in our spiritual lives is part of the rhythm of assurance. Confidence isn't presented to us as a one-time, limited offering from God. We are graced with this gift continuously over a lifetime of growth as we are led toward ever-deepening and demanding levels of faith.

The rhythm of assurance means that we need to continue our spiritual journey of growth whether God is hidden in our hearts or walking openly beside us. "Faith is belief in God *alone*, and therefore it has no props or proofs other than its own inner conviction," wrote Robert Short in *A Time to Be Born—A Time to Die.* "And thus, when God brings a man to stand alone before him as a mature man of faith, God will first hide himself from that man. For when God is hidden, only *faith* in him will then suffice; props and proofs will be of no avail."[10]

This pathway of growth without props and proofs takes us through both shadow and light. Only when we are enveloped by the darkness of our despair can we see those rays of hope leading us back to authentic confidence in God. We cannot perceive the might and glory and love that is God, unless we have known the meaninglessness of life without that mighty, glorious, and loving Presence. The rhythm of assurance repeatedly moves us through the darkness to the Light, from lives filled with the evil fear of despair to lives filled with the fear of God.

A Contemporary Portrait of Confidence

Confidence is only one aspect of the courage we need on our journey toward the loving God we fear and trust; but in certain ways it is the most crucial. If we have the confidence of courage, our lives express our growing faith in God rather than the fear rooted in its absence. With the confidence of courage, we place our belief in God into action during the shadowy and the bright moments of our lives. Whether God is hidden or present, distant or resting in our hearts, we discipline ourselves to exercise the *confidēre* of confidence, to abide with God unceasingly through all the stages of our journey.

In *The Courage to Be*, Paul Tillich wrote at length about an engraving by Albrecht Dürer entitled, "Knight, Death and the Devil," regarded as a classical expression of the spirit of the Protestant Reformation and Luther's courageous confidence. Curious to see this engraving, I finally located a copy of it in a nearby university library and found myself dismayed by the bleakness of the scene. Encased in full armor, a lone knight rides through a dark valley with the figure of death on one side and the devil on the other. With fierce concentration, the knight focuses on the way ahead. "Fearlessly . . . in his solitude, he participates in the power which gives him the courage to affirm himself in spite of the presence of the negativities of existence," Tillich explained. "And his personal confidence is based on a *person-to-person* relationship with God."[11]

Perhaps "Knight, Death and the Devil" expresses the spirit of the Reformation, but I question its accuracy in portraying the confidence of courage in the nuclear age. During the first atomic explosion, we gazed more fully into the face of evil than at any other time in human history. Unlike Dürer's knight, we can't ignore the reality of evil flanking our sides. In the nuclear age, the way of assurance obliges us to do more than fiercely concentrate on God. To attain the assurance that God is always present, always loving, and always holy, we must meet, recognize, and battle the problem of evil, which includes our fear of meaninglessness and the resulting despair we feel.

To gain this confidence of courage, we begin by acknowledging both the evil fear present within the world and that present within our hearts. To believe in God's loving purpose for our lives and to act from that basis, we must discard, rather than don, the armor of Dürer's knight. That which protects the warrior from the evil of the world also harbors the evil that exists within. Our fears, those within and beyond, need to be pulled out of the shadows and scrutinized in full light.

Next we must shed the knight's image of fearlessness. We know evil fear and acknowledge it. Yet that won't banish it from our lives. We need to replace it with a reverence for God instead. To experience reverence, that awe-filled fear of the Almighty missing within the portrait of the knight, we begin by entering into a unique and personal relationship with God, not a person-to-person one. Although we use personal imagery to describe this relationship with the Deity, we realize that the loving God we fear is the Creator beyond all definitions and limits of personhood.

I'm not certain that an engraving expressing the spirit of Christian confidence in the nuclear age exists, but if I were to attempt to create it, I would entitle it "Child, Bomb, and the

Shadow." An androgynous child in a loose-fitting shift and sandals would be kneeling in wonder on a straight road leading through a fertile valley. Both in shadow and light, the child would be raising a lamp high enough overhead to bathe himself or herself, an unveiled nuclear bomb, and the pathway ahead with a supernatural glow. Suffusing the shadows, this holy light would also dispel the darkness that exists here.

The model for this imagined engraving actually lived two millennia ago. Born in an ancient hill town of Judea and raised in another hill town above the fertile valley of southern Galilee, this Child was called "the true light that gives light to every man" (John 1:9). He walked the earth in human form and saw that "men loved darkness instead of light because their deeds were evil" (John 3:19).

Knowing our human helplessness in the face of the evil that exists among and within us, this God-child grew to manhood, ministered, healed, taught, and preached. He also suffered, died, and rose again in order to deliver us from the power of evil. We need only invoke his presence today to affirm the truth of his words: "I am the light of the world. Whoever follows me will never walk in darkness, but will have the light of life" (John 8:12).

With the help of the Son of God, we can raise the lamp of self-knowledge and knowing God on high, discern the evil fear in our lives, and overcome the despair and pervading sense of meaninglessness that evil has created. Our portrayal of the confidence of courage in the nuclear age can be that of a faith-filled child kneeling vulnerably on the fertile road of spiritual growth leading straight to God. Yet this same simple child of faith is capable of confronting the complex reality of fear and evil, symbolized by the atomic bomb and the ever-present shadow of darkness.

Our portrayal of confidence demands much of us as we seek the courage that leads to spiritual wholeness. And it gives much to us in return. The way that leads through despair to hope and confidence teaches us how to live the prayer of assurance fully, a prayer that encompasses both the reality of a meaningful existence and the loving face of God.

When this happens, when our vision is unclouded by the fear that life has no ultimate significance or purpose, we can face the second challenge in answering the divine call to courage. No longer spiritually powerless, we are ready to gain the gentle might of Christ.

II. THE SECOND CHALLENGE
Moving from Weakness to Strength

The Lord is the strength of my life;
of whom shall I be afraid?

(PS. 27:1)

4. Powerlessness

In the Wilderness of Zin, Jesus began his ministry by seeking deeper union with God. Fasting to the limits of his endurance, he lived for forty days and nights alone in the desert. I've often wondered exactly how he filled those hours spent in an area the Old Testament aptly calls Jeshimmon, which means the Devastation.

Down through the centuries, those forty days and nights have been the subject of much speculation: Jesus prayed unceasingly; Jesus surrendered his body and spirit to the Father; Jesus transcended his human limitations; Jesus prepared himself for the superhuman suffering ahead; Jesus was in constant communion with the Father. Although each of these speculations makes good sense, my thoughts about this six weeks tend to be even more pragmatic. Jesus had been led by the Spirit into the land of the Devastation not only to seek and know better the will of his Father but also to figure out how to accomplish what God had given him to do. The very human Jesus, who suffered near starvation in the desert, needed this time of fasting and prayer alone to plan how best to put his Father's demands into action.

At his baptism by John at the Jordan, Jesus had heard God speak in unequivocal terms. Quoting first from the Messiah psalm, God had said of Jesus, "This is my beloved Son" (Ps. 2:7). Next, the Father quoted from the Suffering Servant passages of Isaiah, calling Christ the one "in whom I am well pleased" (Isa. 42:1). When Jesus entered the desolate Wilderness of Zin, he did so as a man proclaimed the chosen Son of God. More startling, he had been told how he, the chosen, was to live and die. No conqueror-king, no religious establishment-ruler, Jesus was to wear the affliction of the Cross rather than the majesty of a crown.

I can't imagine what went through Jesus' mind when he realized that he was to become "despised and rejected by men, a man of sorrows, and familiar with suffering" (Isa. 53:3). This call meant that he would be "pierced by our transgressions" and "crushed for our iniquities" (Isa. 53:4, 5). What must he have thought when he recognized the path God wanted him to follow? Well-schooled in Scripture, Jesus knew, from God's reference to Isaiah, that his fate was to bear "the iniquities of us all," to be "oppressed and afflicted," and "led like a lamb to the slaughter, and as a sheep before her shearers is silent" (Isa. 53:6, 7). Did these prophetic words of Isaiah strike a chord of terror in his heart?

The land of the Devastation very well could have matched the mood of the newly chosen Messiah. How could he feel joy when he had just been told that "it was the Lord's will to crush him and cause him to suffer" and that the Lord would make "his life a guilt offering" (Isa. 53:10). He had been called. He knew his vocation. Bearing our sins, he would be despised, rejected, afflicted, and crushed. He would know unprecedented sorrow and suffering. Silently, showing utter weakness, he would be slaughtered.

And through this display of human powerlessness, he would redeem us. His punishment would bring us peace, and his wounds, healing (Isa. 53:5). He had been called to live and suffer, die and redeem. He was to reject earthly power, worldly prestige and privilege, material security and protection. He was to consider himself as helpless as the sacrificial lambs, who were bound and carried to the temple altar to have their throats slashed in a daily death offering to the Almighty. He was to die so that others might know God. He was to offer himself, helpless and bound, to free those separated from God by sin. He was to be armed only with this suffering in service to humanity.

For forty days and nights, Jesus was alone with God, a fearsome physical hunger, and the terrible burden of this mission. I can't help but think that for those six weeks, Jesus plotted and planned, adopted and discarded methods of action, sought direction and guidance, prayed for strength, questioned his understanding of God's Word, wondered how he could succeed in bringing this peace and healing through suffering as promised in Isaiah, considered options, made contingency plans, pondered the divine will and his all-too-human response.

As his body weakened from lack of food, Jesus' spirit may have grown stronger. As he moved away from a dependence on human needs, he may have moved closer to a dependency on things divine. Encumbered less and less by the physical, he may have lived more and more in the realm of the spirit.

Three Tests of Spiritual Strength

When the forty days came to an end, Jesus encountered a resident of the spiritual world. He met the Evil One, who set up three specific tests of spiritual strength, commonly referred to as the temptations of Jesus. In the Gospel of Matthew, the Greek word *peirazein* is used for "tempt," and its meaning is more complex than a seeking to seduce into evil, which tempting commonly means. As William Barclay, the noted New Testament scholar, writes, *peirazein* "is not meant to make us sin; it is meant to enable us to conquer sin. It is not meant to make us bad, it is meant to make us good. It is not meant to weaken us, it is meant to make us emerge stronger. . . . So, then, we must think of this whole incident, not so much the *tempting*, as the *testing* of Jesus."[1]

On reflection, I didn't find it surprising that Jesus confronted the twin issues of worldly powerlessness and spiritual strength at the end of his days in desert solitude. As he did with Abraham and does with each of us, God tested the depth and quality of his Son's commitment to becoming the Suffering Servant. Through the temptations, Jesus was given a choice. He could confront evil with spiritual power, or he could compromise with Satan for material gain.

In the first test, Satan challenged Jesus, as the chosen Messiah, to use his power selfishly to turn the rocks scattered across the land of the Devastation into bread. Although fast approaching the threshold of starvation, Jesus countered with a lesson that the Old Testament God had taught his people in the wilderness. Reciting from Scripture, Jesus proclaimed that, as humans, we do not live by bread alone, but rather by everything that comes from the mouth of God (Deut. 8:3). Deceptive in its simplicity, Christ's answer clearly explains the way he had chosen. Grounded in a personal relationship with God, his methods would express his complete dependence on the Father to fulfill his spiritual as well as physical hunger.

In the second test, Satan took Jesus to the Temple on the summit of Mount Zion. This time the Evil One stood at the highest point of the temple roof and issued a more sophisticated challenge. Using Scripture itself to trap Jesus, the devil taunted him to throw himself down from the pinnacle to the valley of the Kidron far below, for if he were truly the Son of God, angels, as promised in the Word, would save him from harm. Again, Jesus answered with a lesson the chosen people had been taught centuries ago in the deserts of the Sinai and Negev: "Do not put the Lord your God to the test" (Deut. 6:16). In choosing this particular passage as his response, Jesus was saying that he would follow a path in which divine power was to be held higher than human will. We are the tested, not the testers. We, the powerless, are to trust, not test, the power of God.

The third and last challenge involved the source and use of power once again. On a mountaintop, Jesus and Satan surveyed the splendors of all the kingdoms of this world. Here the devil made his final attack, offering Jesus all that he saw, if only he'd bow down and worship him. Returning to yet another lesson taught to the chosen people of God wandering in the wilderness, Jesus replied, "Away from me, Satan! For it is written: 'Worship the Lord your God, and serve him only' " (Deut. 6:13). The spiritual pathway that would bear his name wouldn't lead to compromise with evil, wouldn't come to terms with the world, or ask that we become like the world. Instead, we are led to adopt methods that confront evil, bring God's terms to the world, and change the world with these divine demands.

In each testing, Jesus made clear that the spiritual always comes before the physical, the will of God before human will, the power of God before worldly power, spiritual strength before human might. Yet the methods we need to adopt in order to exist in this spiritual realm are ones demanding that we become dependent, powerless, and weak in worldly terms. We must allow ourselves to be helpless, to suffer, to know pain, and to die to our most fundamental drive—the urge for power and control over our lives.

In the three testings of Christ, we see that we are being asked to depend on Another, to trust without any hope of gaining worldly power, and to worship despite our suffering. It's a path somewhat familiar to us now, one we began to walk when we confronted the evil of meaninglessness and despair in our lives. Seeking, encountering, and deepening our communion with God, we grew in dependency, trust, and reverence. Our hope and belief in the world of the Spirit slowly replaced our fear centering on a world devoid of God, and we struggled to learn the confidence of this new spiritual courage growing within us.

The Fear of Powerlessness

Taking the next step along the pathway toward courage, we find ourselves facing, once again, the evilness of fear working in our lives. This time, the aspect of evil fear that threatens our relationship with God, ourselves, and others is our fear of being powerless.

Dedicated to living our lives more confidently in the spiritual realm, we discover that more is demanded of us, not less. Following our baptism into the confidence of courage, we are asked to become suffering servants and embrace pain and loss in our lives. While basking in our assurance of God's purpose for our lives, we reluctantly waken to the divine demand to grow strong in God's purpose. Unfortunately, we most often react to this new demand as Elijah did. Displaying the confidence of courage, he overcame the evil fear of despair to defeat the prophets of Baal on Mount Carmel (1 Kings 18:17–40). Yet almost directly afterward he received threats from a wrathful Jezebel, grew afraid, and ran for his life to Beer-sheba in Judah (1 Kings 19:3).

Knowing God and gaining confidence, we approach the next stage in our journey toward courage and realize that, like Jesus, we are being tested by the Evil One, and that, like Elijah, our spirits are ridden by the evil fear of our own human and spiritual powerlessness. We dislike feeling weak and impotent. We don't want to experience pain, suffering, or loss. Yet, after we move from despair through hope to confidence, we find that we must commit ourselves to being powerless in this world, which also means being willing to embrace that very pain, suffering, and loss we fear most in this life.

I suspect that death is the unspoken word at the core of our fear, for nothing brings home the fact of our powerlessness in life as much as our dying. This death we fear begins with our awareness of our own mortality and extends to include the dying that takes place daily in our lives as we travel closer to God. We discover that living in union with God requires us to die over and over again to all that is keeping us separated from the Creator. To live in the spiritual realm, we must die to the attachments of this world. To live a life in the Spirit, we must die to the spirit of self. To approach the wholeness for which we were created, we must die to the inner drives toward evil. To become Christlike, we must die to our fear of suffering, pain, and loss. "In fact, every command of Jesus is a call to die," Dietrich Bonhoeffer wrote in *The Cost of Discipleship*.[2]

Too often we ignore this call. We don't want to face our physical death, much less the daily dying that Christ demands. Although the cross is everywhere—on steeples, in our church sanctuaries, on Bible covers, and bumper stickers—we see but don't live its message. Worn as jewelry, fashioned into floral wreaths, even decorating light-switch plates and underwear, the cross has become one of the most readily recognized symbols in late-twentieth-century Western civilization. Yet when we see it, our usual knee-jerk reaction is to automatically state, "Christ suffered and died on the Cross for our sins," without adding our responsibility to bear our own crosses. Although humbled and awed by Jesus' supreme act of sacrifice, we don't dare to search beyond our purely dogmatic response to the reality of his life, teachings, and death.

"The Cross as dogma is painless speculation," The Quaker writer Thomas Kelly bluntly reminded us before adding, "the Cross as lived suffering is anguish and glory."[3] We are called to share Christ's suffering and death by carrying our individual crosses, made of all that must die within, so that we may live in deeper union with God.

The cross is the universally understood symbol of Christianity, but the demands of the Creator that we live in a closer and more constant communion with him transcend religious boundaries. On our spiritual journey from fear to courage, we should have no difficulty understanding Mahatma Gandhi's statement that "devotion is not mere lip-worship, it is a wrestling with death."[4] Called to devote ourselves to the Cross, we now must wrestle with dying to self, to the world, to evil and sin. Yet everything in our human nature struggles against embracing these pain-filled deaths, for to submit to them is to submit our lives, in their entirety, to a Power we can neither comprehend nor control.

Ironically, our U.S. society that today advertises the cross on everything from earrings to bookmarks is the same culture that numbers itself among the most fearful about death. We fear mass nuclear annihilation and a collective moral one of the soul. We fear a violent end to our lives in the decaying landscapes of our cities and on the darkened highways of our countryside. We fear deadly epidemics, terminal diseases, acts of God, and natural calamities. We fear drunk drivers, serial murderers, AIDS carriers, malfunctioning O-ring seals, and earthquakes. We use euphemisms both for the legal, immoral taking of life and for the act of dying. We place our aged in death centers far removed from the intercourse of daily living. Letting death replace sex as the great unmentionable, we do our best to confine it to the impersonal, anesthetized, and antiseptic isolation of the hospital room.

The fear that distances us emotionally from physical death is the same fear that prevents us from wrestling with the daily dying of self necessary for spiritual growth. We fear what we cannot control. Despite all our efforts, our bodies will ultimately decay, and we will die. Similarly, if we heed the call to the Cross, we will die again and again on more demanding levels of self. In either case, we are powerless to stop the process of dying. Power is in the hands of Another.

In a workshop with hospice workers, a young woman answered, with an astute observation, one of my queries about what it meant to heed the call to the Cross today. She noted that when a person carries a cross, that person can move in only one direction at a time. Similarly, when placed on a cross to die, a person can face in only one direction and is powerless to change that direction. In dying and death, it is not possible to confront the cross itself. Instead, the dying person looks toward the one who first put the cross on his or her shoulders and then raised him or her up on it.

This image stayed with me for months after the workshop, for it accurately reflects Jesus' position at Calvary. The Crucifixion speaks of utter and complete submission, in which the issue of control has already been resolved. Jesus chose to suffer, to sacrifice, to surrender, and to die. Fear wasn't a factor; the choice had been made. Heeding the call to the Cross, the Messiah had expressed the confidence of courage in accepting God's purpose for his life. Being nailed to the cross, Jesus had exhibited the strength of courage in submitting to God's will for his death. No fear of his human powerlessness obscured his vision. Choosing to let God control his life and death, Christ faced his Father free from the evilness of fear based on human and spiritual weakness.

The Arrogance of Disobedience

Unfortunately, this inspiring picture of a subservient Christ is emotionally distant from our typical human response to the fear of powerlessness in our lives. When we encounter any aspect of this evil fear, our reaction generally falls into one of three categories: we disregard God, we feel insecure in relation to God, or we abandon God.

Each response has its source in the arrogance of disobedience. We believe, but we refuse to strengthen our belief through obedience. The confidence of courage, which is grounded in our belief in God, isn't accompanied by the gentle spiritual might of courage, which is grounded in our complete obedience to God. When the evil fear of powerlessness makes its appearance in our lives, we choose to pridefully disobey God's will rather than confront the crosses we are called to bear.

In the second movement toward courage, we realize that disobedience is easier than accepting Christ's call to suffer, to know pain, and to experience loss and death. The nineteenth-century Danish philosopher, Søren Kierkegaard, rightly concluded that we find it so hard to believe because we find it so hard to obey. Until we learn obedience, we cannot retain the confidence of courage nor can we develop the second cornerstone of courage, spiritual strength.

Disregarding God

On gaining the confidence of courage, we feel a well-ordered sureness and harmony. Through our initial communion with God, we are certain of the Almighty's presence and purpose in our lives and in the world. We are learning to pray and live a rudimentary Christian life. After wandering in the spiritual wilderness, we have reached a comfortable plateau where we think we are in total control of our lives. But this pleasant state is illusory. To grow is to travel from this nondemanding and fear-denying place through a landscape filled with demands that we surrender our power and control to God and face the full evilness of our fear.

In *The Interior Castle*, Saint Teresa of Avila considered this stage as the third of seven dwelling places on our journey to God at the center of the castle. It is a place with which she was most familiar since, by her own admission, she spent eighteen years of her life wrongly disregarding God's demands to surrender.

Although leading good lives, we—who have a similar need for control—have not allowed ourselves to let go of self and abandon ourselves to God. We choose to do our will, not God's, to become entrenched in this pleasant niche rather than admit to our own powerlessness in following Christ's call.

Saint Teresa makes it clear that no matter how hard we try, we cannot remain on this plateau. We are not and never have been in control. In spite of our attempts to disregard the will of God, life continues, and change occurs. To exist is to experience transformation that growing in Christ demands of us.

"It is no easy process of change but is fraught with crises," Father Christopher Bryant stated. "For a change in the seat of control within the personality takes place."[5] With the arrogance of disobedience, we may believe we are placing ourselves securely in that seat of control. We may actually succeed in temporarily diverting or thwarting God's purpose for our lives, but we cannot stop the process of transformation from happening. God continues to work within us, inexorably challenging us to loosen our tight hold on self and to recognize our human helplessness.

Less than half a mile from my present home in eastern North Carolina, the Roanoke River appears to meander along the edge of town, flat, broad, wide, and deep. At first glance, it seems to have none of the raw, unharnessed power of the river that flows through the mountain village I called home in New Mexico. Instead, the deceptively placid Roanoke is the embodiment of control, safely held in check by a series of levees and dams upstream. To my surprise, after the recent ice storms and rain, I discovered the truth about the Roanoke, whose name literally means "river of death." Swollen with the spring runoff, the river became transformed, changing, if only for a few hours, from stately to turbulent, driven by an unseen and ever-present power easily disregarded under more pleasant circumstances. Similarly, even when we ignore God's call, that unseen Presence powering our lives brings us face to face with the painful crises of change and reminds us once again Who is in control.

Insecurity with God

When we encounter any of the constellation of fears clustered around our powerlessness over pain, suffering, and loss, we frequently respond in a second disobedient way: we relate to God with insecurity. When we gained the confidence of courage, we moved through doubting to hoping and confiding in a loving, personal God. Yet we mistakenly believe that we will feel God's presence throughout the difficult and easier moments of our lives.

As we grow spiritually, we soon discover moments when God is silent in our hearts. Too often, we mistake that silence for absence, which only increases our fear that perhaps the Almighty has abandoned us to the pain that we, as broken people separated from God, suffer in a world filled with other broken and pain-filled people.

Despite our obvious need, God seems strangely removed from our lives, as though deliberately withholding the comfort of the Divine Presence from us. Disquiet starts to undermine our certainty that God is both personal and ever-present. As we ponder this growing distance between the Creator and created, our prayers grow stilted and dry. We begin to speak words of trust with our lips, not our hearts, for our insecure hearts contain questions about the reality behind these familiar phrases. Finding that the psalmist similarly struggled to maintain a secure relationship with God gives us little consolation. We don't care to know that approximately three thousand years ago, a man of God had cried the same self-pitying, untrusting refrain:

> How long, O Lord? Will you forget me forever?
> How long will you hide your face from me?
> How long must I wrestle with my thoughts and every day have
>   sorrow in my heart?
> How long . . . ?
>
> (PS. 13:1–3)

In the silence, we hear no answers. We are deeply disturbed by God's seeming abandonment of us. With the arrogance of disobedience, we react by refusing to believe fully in Christ's promise to be with us always, even to the very end of the age (Matt. 28:20). Feeling forsaken by the Creator, we question the validity of Moses' speech to Joshua, charging him to lead the people of Israel out of the wilderness. Reading Moses' words, we have trouble accepting his advice:

> Be strong and courageous. Do not be afraid or terrified . . . for the Lord your God goes with you; he will never leave you nor forsake you. Do not be afraid; do not be discouraged.
>
> (Deut. 31:7–9)

We are afraid. We know discouragement. We feel alone and fear that the Lord our God doesn't go with us. Refusing to trust, we choose to live lives in disobedience to both God's word and Christ's promise.

Abandoning God

It is but a short step from losing trust in God's presence to forsaking God. In this third response of disobedience to the

Creator, our fear that we have been forsaken is replaced by anger and bitterness over our apparent abandonment. Just when we need to feel God's presence and a sure sense of divine purpose for our lives, the Almighty has left us to suffer mental and physical anguish alone, to know pain, grief, and loss alone, to experience the very real misery and vulnerability of earthly existence alone.

Such a perception of an absent, impersonal, noncaring, and noncontrolling Creator fills us with rage. Deprived of both divine purpose and presence, we allow this anger to turn into bitterness toward the One who created us. We refuse to follow a God who cannot help us make sense of our suffering, pain, and loss. We will not obey a God who won't control the evil of senseless and hopeless suffering in this world. Nor will we accept the commands of a God who cannot help us overcome or control suffering in our lives.

Here we reach the nadir of human arrogance, daring God to justify divine existence and to explain divine actions to us before we'll believe and obey. Created for wholeness, we instead have fractured our relationship with God and with our selves. We are farther away from gaining courage rather than closer, more distant from spiritual strength than nearer. We are powerless and cannot accept it; we also refuse to admit to God's power over our lives. Struggling to come to terms with the painful reality of human existence, we have cut ourselves off from the Creator of all life. Through our fear of being weak and powerless, we have removed ourselves from the Source of all power.

The Only Alternative

Writing this chapter on the fear of powerlessness, I have forced myself to remember, once again, the most recent occasion when I chose to walk this prideful, disobedient path away from God. It occurred during the prolonged suffering and dying of a dear young friend, who had lived few years but lived deeply in the life of the spirit. Recalling those insecure, angry, bitter, God-forsaking moments, I am shocked at how easily I distanced myself from self, others, and God as I allowed fear to control my life. Responding to close personal loss with disobedience, I experienced both the darkness that comes with such pain and the evil that exists at the heart of fear.

Justifications and rationalizations abound for behavior such as mine. We seem to have so few mechanisms to cope with unjust pain, needless suffering, the grief of loss, or the mystery of dying. We can find even fewer answers to our helpless, heartbroken cry to God, "Why?" Trying to reconcile suffering or death, which is our human condition, with a just, loving, personal, all-good, all-powerful, all-wise God becomes a fruitless task. We soon discover that there are no answers to our "Why?" unless we make God unjust, unloving, impersonal, and flawed in terms of goodness, power, and wisdom. In doing this, we define God as less than the God in ultimate control of all creation. We mold God anew on the human scale, finite, limited, in charge of neither good nor evil, which is not the God revealed in the Scriptures, in the person of Jesus Christ, and in the powerful workings of the Holy Spirit. We have substituted the relative for the Absolute, the situational for the Ultimate. And we have come no closer to answering why we suffer and die, and—equally important—why we are powerless to control both suffering and dying.

We can fall back on a raw faith and trust in the revealed God and rest, for a time, in the relative safety of the *confidēre* of courage. Yet the only alternative left to us, as children of God, is to proceed toward the strength of courage where we accept our human powerlessness and surrender fully to the power of God. If we are to grow, we have no choice but to explore the new terrain around this second cornerstone of courage, a terrain leading us directly into the transforming fires of surrender that alone produce gentle might.

5. Surrender

Although faith and trust carry us far, we need the endurance of strength to complete our spiritual journey toward courage. Like physical strength, the strength of courage is developed through a disciplined training of body, mind, and spirit. We begin these exercises by moving past the conundrum of "Why?" questions, which surround our fear of being powerless, to center on "How?" questions, which help us develop the strength of courage. Only by exploring the "How?" of suffering, loss, and death will we learn to deal with the evil fear of powerlessness and transform it into the gentle strength of courage.

Consider, for a moment, the futility of questioning "Why?" a futility aptly revealed in the Book of Job. Perhaps no other story in the Old Testament has been argued and interpreted from so many conflicting perspectives over time. It's not my intention to write a commentary on this challenging book or to express my theology regarding the nature of God, as was done in a disturbing, yet surprisingly well-received bestseller.[1]

Walking along the spiritual path of growth, we will find few answers to dogmatic questions arising from a religious or scientific world view. On the spiritual path to courage specifically, we will be given no satisfactory answers to why the innocent suffer. All we know with certainty is that we won't discover the precise nature of the Creator or creation in this life. Until we continue our life journey through death, we can rely only on conjecture.

Although we struggle to understand the attributes and motivations of God in light of our painful experiences, we soon learn that it's a fruitless task. Like Job, we discover that all human answers to "Why?" questions are partial and unsatisfactory. Perhaps suffering may be a divine test, a form of disciplining, a punishment, or any combination thereof. But in fully accepting any of these answers, we find no way to reconcile the unjust suffering of innocents with our limited knowledge and understanding of who and what God is. We cannot place the birth of severely handicapped children, the mindless tragedies experienced by millions of godly people, even God's cruelty toward the righteous Job into any reasonable context and still call God all-good and all-powerful.

We have run into a theological dead end. If God is not in ultimate control, can God truly be divine? And if God is a good, just, loving, personal God, how do we explain suffering, pain, and loss?

New Questions

I don't believe we need to find a new perspective on the question of suffering; we need new questions instead. But to pose these questions we must look beyond the Old Testament God, who promises the coming of the Messiah and closes his Word with a curse (Mal. 4:3). We must begin by looking at the historical reality of the New Testament Jesus, who fulfills his Father's promise and closes his life by surrendering it in a sacrifice of love.

In Christ, the question of God's power over evil transcends uncertainty and conjecture. In Christ's life, teachings, death, and resurrection, we are given genuine, objective evidence of God's love conquering the full onslaught of evil. Through the loving sacrifice of Christ, we find answers, not to why suffering, pain, loss, and dying exist, but to how we may become free from our fear of these very things.

Our focus changes from why an all-powerful, all-good God creates suffering to how we must deal with this humanly unexplainable conflict central to the spiritual life. Recognizing that we have no tidy theories, no comforting answers, no wise and compassionate explanations, we stop saying "Why?" to God's design and start looking at how we are a part of that design. Instead of questioning why God is important to us, we ask how we are important to God.

With our "Why?" questions, we are trying to place self, not God, at the center of our universe. We are focusing on our needs and pain, while refusing to acknowledge the rightful Center. Being made in the image of God, we dare to think that we can grasp the total reality of our Creator.

Yet we must realize the senselessness of such an effort. Out of the whirlwind of the storm, the Lord chose to answer Job's "Why?" with telling questions of his own. God's queries underscored how little Job knew about the nature and workings of the divine. In the end, Job recognized that he had scarcely any knowledge of the Lord, making his demand to know why he suffered both unreasonable and foolish. Our demands to know why we suffer are equally ludicrous. We need to approach the Almighty with questions whose answers can be found and lived during our earthly journey between birth and death:

- How do you work in my life?
- How do you want me to be?
- How do I listen and learn?
- How do you want me to act?
- How do I become more Christlike?
- How do I grow through this suffering?

Our attitudes about suffering become more important than the affliction itself. Since we won't receive satisfactory reasons for our suffering, we need to learn good responses to it. Instead of seeking explanations, as I did when my dear friend died a painful death, we can discipline ourselves to respond to such senseless tragedies in a spiritual manner coming from the depths of our characters. We need to stop and hear God's voice, accept what the Almighty is telling us through this particular suffering, and obey that lesson with a maturity grounded in the Spirit.

The Godly Response

Few things are harder to achieve than this godly response. In *New Seeds of Contemplation*, Thomas Merton defined it as the "perfect abandonment to the will of God in things you cannot control, and perfect obedience to Him in everything that depends on your own volition, so that in all things, in your interior life and in your outward works for God, you desire only one thing, which is the fulfillment of His will."[2]

Our natural inclination is to turn to the Lord when we need help. But it is also natural for us to turn away from God when suffering continues. "Beware of turning to evil, which you prefer to affliction," Elihu wisely warned Job (Job 36:21). We, too, find it easier to succumb to destructive bitterness, frustration, and anger than to accept our powerlessness, our limited understanding, and the seeming unfairness of suffering. It's much more satisfying to hurl our anger at God than to quietly ask God to help us with our anguish.

Although bitterness, frustration, and anger are legitimate human responses to suffering and the fear of being weak, how we choose to deal with these feelings is the key to our continued spiritual growth. If we commit ourselves to doing God's will, we can turn to the Almighty with our bitter, frustrated, and angry feelings and seek divine help in accepting them as part of the human condition. Only then are we using our feelings constructively. Rather than protesting our condition or insisting on explanations, we are acknowledging that suffering and all its attendant feelings and fears are under the direction and domain of God.

In choosing the godly response, we choose to experience what suffering means, what it has to teach us, and what its purpose is in our lives. We find that we are called to examine and use suffering positively. Time and again, while I struggled to come to terms with my friend's death, I would turn to the journals of Katherine Mansfield for solace. Her courageous words shone like a beacon, pointing the way through the darkness of my grief and anguish toward this difficult godly response of abandonment and obedience to God's will.

Born in New Zealand in 1888, Katherine Mansfield completed her education in England and soon became part of the literary world of London. Blessed with both delicate beauty and considerable writing talent, Mansfield seemed unaware of the former and never developed the full potential of the latter. After suffering acutely from pleurisy and tuberculosis, she died at the age of thirty-four, leaving a rich legacy of short stories, letters, and a personal journal.

It was in her personal journal that I discovered this pathway leading from the evil fear of weakness to the transformation that brings the gentle strength of courage. Mansfield wrote in one journal entry:

I do not want to die without leaving a record of my belief that suffering can be overcome. For I do believe it. What must one do? There is no question of what is called "passing beyond it." This is false. One must *submit*. Do not resist. Take it. Be overwhelmed. Accept it fully. Make it *part of life*. Everything in life that we really accept undergoes a change. So suffering must become Love. This is the mystery. This is what I must do. I must pass from personal love to greater love. I must give to the whole of life what I gave to one. . . .

She next wrote of how her doctor helped her to bear pain by suggesting that ill health was a repairing process, an idea that challenged her:

If "suffering" is not a repairing process, I will make it so. I will learn the lesson it teaches. . . . It is to lose oneself more utterly, to love more deeply, to feel oneself part of life,—not separate. Oh Life! accept me—make me worthy—teach me.

And then with a breath-catching poignancy, she added:

I write that. I look up. The leaves move in the garden, the sky is pale, and I catch myself weeping. It is hard—it is hard to make a good death.[3]

When we submit to suffering, accept our own powerlessness, listen to God's voice speaking out of the painful experience, and struggle to obey the divine lesson we hear, we begin to live our answer to the "How?" questions we've asked. We experience firsthand what Katherine Mansfield expressed so movingly—that our God is an infinite God of love, who is willing to help us move through and beyond all afflictions. We understand, at last, God's love for us, which was most clearly portrayed through the suffering of Christ on the cross. Suffering transformed into love becomes Mansfield's "repairing process," making it a source of healing both in our broken lives and in the fractured world in which we live.

Other Voices from the Past

How do we submit to the reality of suffering in our lives and learn to transform it into love? Again, Katherine Mansfield shows us the way with her heart-wrenching confession: "It is hard to make a good death."

The rich heritage of Christian death journals may seem a strange starting point for those of us raised in late twentieth-century America. We live in a death-denying society and tend to think it bizarre to dwell on how to suffer and die well. Yet pamphlets on the art of dying were among the first printed books in western Europe. From the sixteenth to the nineteenth century, devotional writers of the Christian faith attached great importance to recording deathbed sayings, for they felt that the dying person was "waiting in the grand foyer of glory."

A good death to these writers meant facing death with the certainty of God's love and the strength of courage. It meant a graceful dying out of suffering and loss into health and life anew. In that spirit, John Wesley proudly exclaimed, "Our people die well!"

Good dying was perhaps presented best in the final scene of John Bunyan's *Pilgrim's Progress*. Approaching the Celestial City, Mr. Standfast pauses, as he is crossing the river of death, to say, "This river has been a terror to many; yea, the thoughts of it also have often frightened me. . . . I see myself now at the end of my journey; my toilsome days are ended."

Mr. Standfast next speaks lovingly of the Lord he has longed to see and hear: "He has held me and kept me from mine iniquities; yea, my steps have been strengthened in his way."[4]

With that, Mr. Standfast ceases to be seen, but the regions above the beautiful gate of the city are filled with horses and chariots, trumpeters and pipers, singers and musicians, welcoming the pilgrims home.

We in America have lost much of this loving confidence and joyful strength in the face of suffering and death. We would be shocked to see a book outlining the discipline of "fore-fancying your deathbed" such as Alexander Whyte wrote, or one with the title *A Salve for a Sicke Man (The Right Way of Dying Well)*, another popular pamphlet written by the Puritan, William Perkins. Even the classic *Pilgrim's Progress* is considered little more than a relic from bygone days, filled with antiquated language and values.

I must confess that I, too, held that view until I entered graduate school. During my second year, I worked as a research assistant on a project examining American female relationships. My selected readings included the letters and journals of the wives and daughters of missionaries sent to the Western states during the last half of the nineteenth century. At first, I found reading this material a morbid exercise, since the women appeared to write almost exclusively about ill health, suffering, and dying. The primitive state of medicine, the scientific ignorance, and the seemingly endless cataloguing of ills tended to obscure the more important messages left by these women.

Only after several weeks' immersion in their writings did I realize I had grown familiar with their world view. For them, illness and death took place in the mainstream of life. Although they voiced fear over suffering, they accepted pain, illness, and death as integral parts of living. On intimate terms with the process of dying well, these women acknowledged their powerlessness, accepted suffering, and usually experienced it with a strong and courageous dignity.

I forget now what information I gleaned for the project, but I vividly remember the spiritual strength of these pioneer women. They rarely asked "Why?" of God. Instead, they sought to make their powerlessness, their suffering, and death a meaningful part of life. Submitting to and accepting the unacceptable, they drained evil of its power and let love take its place. Surrendering with grace, they moved through and beyond fear to the quiet strength of courage.

Two Images of Transformation

Much of what I have written in this chapter deals with our spiritual responses and attitudes toward the evil fear of being powerless in the face of suffering and death. Yet no examination of suffering would be complete without a brief look at the writings of two sixteenth-century Carmelite Spanish mystics and friends, Saint Teresa of Avila and Saint John of the Cross. With acute psychological insight, they understood how the inner journey to God, wholeness, and courage involves a continuing series of transformations requiring a surrendering of self.

In *The Interior Castle*, Teresa used the metamorphosis of the butterfly to express the change we experience as we draw ever nearer to God. She saw us as silkworms, beginning each transformation in pain. After constructing a cocoon and confronting the darkness within, the silkworm undergoes a mysterious change to emerge, with strength, into new life as the butterfly. Teresa felt that transformation involves the dying of evil and the birth of goodness, which mirrors, over and over, the mystery of Christ's death and resurrection.

Saint John of the Cross used a different image to portray the transformation we experience on our Christian journey toward courage. He likened it to the night and divided it into three parts: twilight, midnight, and dawn. Twilight is the night of the senses; midnight, the night of the spirit; and dawn, the time of union with God.

Saint John's celebrated *Dark Night of the Soul*, parallels Saint Teresa's butterfly imagery. In both, we are immersed in the pain of powerlessness and tested by our evil fears before a mysterious power molds us anew. Remaining active yet passive, we prepare ourselves for transformation by actively surrendering any desires and impulses contrary to our consciously held ideal of Christlike behavior. Yet when change does occur, when suffering and surrender become Mansfield's "repairing process," it comes from beyond us as a gift from God, neither summoned nor commanded.

From these two images, we see that a spiritual force, which we call God, is guiding us through the transformation that leads from weakness through surrender to the gentle Christlike strength of courage. These two Spanish mystics knew that the experience of God is no mere intellectual knowledge. It is something we experience with body and soul, emotion and instinct, intuition and heart. In darkness and in light, God is present, directing us from within.

The God of grace, who draws us to seek and find the Divine Presence in order to learn the confidence of courage, now helps us transcend our fear of powerlessness in order to gain the strength of courage. "The believer who can see the forces of change at work in him as the summons of the same God who disclosed himself in the man of Nazareth is strengthened and reassured," wrote Christopher Bryant in *Jung and the Christian Way.* "He can understand the pressures as the voice of Christ saying 'Follow me' and 'Fear not, only believe.' His reliance on Christ will foster the courage and steadfastness he needs to fulfill his destiny."[5]

To fulfill our destiny—to develop the strength of courage— we enter the darkness of the cocoon and surrender the fear that inhibits our growth. We submit to the Dark Night of the Soul, confident that we will emerge transformed by the Spirit and filled with spiritual power.

The Furnace of Transformation

To be transformed is to undergo a life-and-death struggle with the evil potential existing within each of us. At first glance, this description of transformation may sound rather melodramatic, but I assure you, it is not! Examining the evil fear of powerlessness underlying our attitudes and responses to suffering means battling our frightened and false selves that refuse to surrender power and control totally and unconditionally to the Lord Jesus Christ.

Through the drama of the Resurrection, Christ proved that only he can overcome the power of evil. And only in and through him can we survive the trial of transformation that changes us from fearing our weakness before God to being filled with spiritual strength. Transformation becomes a process in which we struggle to be purified of all but Christ, who is our truest self.

Entering Saint Teresa's cocoon or Saint John's Dark Night, we come face to face with our fear of powerlessness, our potential for evil, and our falseness. We encounter these very real aspects of self, but we do not totally destroy them. The cocoon and dark night convey a place of change, one in which the power of evil is overcome and our false selves are transformed into the true one in Christ. It becomes an act of personal purification, in which we willingly sacrifice ourselves so that we may be changed from fearful to strong, from fragmented to whole.

Through the strength of the Spirit, we are able to participate in this painful process, which is so much like the baptism with fire that John the Baptist promised us the Messiah would bring (Matt. 3:11). In the furnace of change, our evil is burnt away and the good is left cleansed, strengthened, and tempered by the purifying flame of Christ. Emerging from the furnace, we integrate these purified parts of ourselves and are delivered from those unredeemable aspects of evil within.

We have become Saint Teresa's butterfly in all its newfound freedom and beauty. We are glorious rays of the dawn's first light, shining brightly after the darkness of the night of the senses and spirit. Yet we barely reflect that creative Love, who continues to illuminate our darkest corners, fuel our personal furnaces of transformation, and heal the evil within us and beyond.

To move from evil to good, from fear to courage, and from powerlessness to strength, we must become engaged in this continuous cycle of suffering, sacrificing, surrendering, and healing. When we begin to trust this transforming movement that reenacts the mystery of the Cross and Resurrection, we find ourselves ready to learn those practices that keep us free from the fear of powerlessness while building the gentle strength of courage.

6. Gentle Might

To transform our fear of being powerless into spiritual strength, we stopped focusing on the reasons for our suffering and began to explore options for responding positively to it. Not just what we endure but how well we choose to endure defines this mysterious transformation of the spirit.

Having survived the soul-fires of surrender, we now recognize our God-given ability to find creative ways to grow ever stronger in our painful encounters with suffering and death. As we move away from fear-induced weaknesses, we dare to dream, investigate, and experiment. No longer imprisoned by our fear of powerlessness, we experience a freedom that is exhilarating in its newness. An entirely unsuspected dimension of life opens up within us. We feel the Divine Presence as never before. Familiar yet different, God creates a quiet place in our hearts, where we feel assured, secure, and increasingly liberated from the paralyzing grip of fear.

Our creative energy is nourished in that place of quiet. There we have a chance to renew our imaginative qualities and explore our potential to innovate, invent, and produce. Changed, we desire to work change itself into the fabric of our daily lives. We seek to worship the Lord, understand ourselves, and relate to our neighbors with a fertile freedom arising out of that quiet, secure place within.

Of all the creative qualities that are ours to develop, I have found three that are crucial in our search to gain the strength of courage. Learning curiosity, wisdom, and joy becomes essential to our quest at this stage. Quite frankly, without these qualities, the strength of courage cannot be attained. With them, we are able to move closer to the wholeness for which we strive.

On the surface, curiosity, wisdom, and joy sound like wonderful qualities to possess. Who, at one time or another, hasn't enjoyed the fruits of a lively imagination, constructive knowledge, or a holy happiness? Yet to possess these three creative qualities, we must experience pain beyond what we felt during our transformation. Physical strength builds on friction and requires the constant challenge of disciplined exercising to maintain or increase the level of strength. Similarly, spiritual strength builds on the painful friction of creativity and requires the disciplined exercising of curiosity, wisdom, and joy to maintain or increase the strength of our spirits.

As with any strengthening exercise, we must be ready to face both hard work and overwhelming internal and external resistance. In *The Road Less Traveled*, M. Scott Peck astutely equated evil with laziness. We humans are loath to experience the pain inherent in spiritual growth and will go to great, and even absurd, lengths to avoid or escape it. Yet, in our very avoidance, we sow the seeds for greater pain and stunted growth. We must learn to engage our spiritual muscles and test them to their limits. We need to push ourselves in the spiritual realm to the outer edges of our endurance. When we most want to retreat, we must discipline ourselves to advance by exercising our curiosity, wisdom, and joy.

After the death of my close friend Deanna, I forgot this basic lesson in the strength of courage. I knew and trusted what God had done for me in the past. I also had hope and confidence in what God would do in the future. But now, in the present, I could see no further than the needless and unjust suffering that was part of my grief.

I knew instinctively that confidence in a past and future God was not enough. I needed to experience and trust my Creator in the present moment of suffering. I had to face the Almighty, who speaks to us in the present tense and defines all that is divine in terms of bygone days, times yet to come, *and* the here and now. "I AM WHO I AM," God thundered from a burning bush to Moses (Ex. 3:14). "I am with you always," the resurrected Christ assured his disciples (Matt. 28:20).

Slowly I reestablished communion with the God of the burning bush and the gentler Christ. As I grew more confident of God in the present moment, my "Why?" questions turned to "How?" I cannot say strongly enough how important Bible study, devotional reading, and prayer became to me. They opened onto a path that led me away from my fear of being powerless and pointed me toward that second cornerstone of courage, strength. But I didn't experience this strength of courage until some months after Deanna's death. And this healing strength sprang from an unexpected source—my dreams.

I consider dreams one of the ways in which God makes the divine will known to us, a view shared by the ancient prophets, the early Christians, and an increasing number of spiritual seekers again today. Since I was first introduced to depth psychology nearly twenty years ago, I've written daily in a personal journal, frequently including accounts of my dreams.

During Deanna's dying and in the weeks following her death, prayer and study came somewhat easily. But I had to force myself to write in my journal, and I could no longer remember my dreams. Then one morning I awoke with tears wetting my pillow and a quiet joy growing within my heart. With no difficulty, I remembered what I had dreamed. Deanna stood before me, not as she was during her illness, but healthy and glowing and whole. Words weren't necessary, for in the luminous air she smiled reassuringly and radiated a wondrous serenity that filled me with the peace that had been missing throughout those long months of darkness.

I sensed that, after opening myself to the Lord and the spiritual power of change, I had been led to depths within myself where my God-given ability to be creative worked to help me move through my pain, loss, and sorrow. A close reading of C. G. Jung's *Memories, Dreams, Reflections* verified the accuracy of this feeling. Jung theorized that our dreams anticipate our potential wholeness while compensating for neglected areas of our lives. By confronting us with deeper levels of self, dreams can become sources of insight, energy, and healing, much as my dream of Deanna had.

Our search for wholeness is compatible with our search for union with God. The second-century Christian bishop Irenaeus understood this intuitively, for he wrote that "the glory of God is man fully alive." Working with our dreams is only one of the many creative ways we can become wholly alive.

In learning to develop curiosity, wisdom, and joy, we can discover new approaches to coping with our pain, to healing the wounds made by our suffering and the suffering of others, and to resting peacefully and securely in the Lord's presence. We also find constructive ways to uncover our fear of powerlessness, come to terms with it, and replace it with the sure knowledge that a powerful God does direct and guide our lives. Giving expression to creative forces deep within, ultimately, empowers us. To tap this powerful, healing energy, we begin by examining our potential to be curious.

Curiosity

A basic creative quality, curiosity centers on the questions we have about our search for wholeness and for God. Being curious means that we are seeking answers within and beyond us as to the nature and workings of the human and the divine. A God-given trait, curiosity needs to be constantly practiced to become fully developed. Although as children we have a great deal of curiosity, we too often lose this ability to question creatively as we grow older.

One of my favorite incidents in the Gospel of Matthew is when Jesus ignored the disciples' overprotective concern for him and warmly welcomed youngsters into his presence, saying, "Let the little children come to me, and do not hinder them, for the kingdom of heaven belongs to such as these" (Matt. 19:14). Then he placed his hands on them, hands that conferred both divine blessing and healing. Through this small story, I am reminded once again that children, in their simplicity and their curiosity, are near to God and to the lost likeness of Christ himself.

As adults, we need not lose our curiosity, which is so fundamental to our ability to be creative. The ways in which we can develop curiosity are virtually unlimited. But to gain spiritual strength through creativity, we need to exercise our curiosity in three distinct areas: by daydreaming, by recording and exploring our dreams, and by building a lively imagination through painting, drawing, sculpting, drama, making music, or writing.

Contrary to popular opinion, the first exercise, daydreaming, is not a wool-gathering waste of time, *if* we do it in a mature, disciplined fashion. We take the first step by daring to think of ourselves as spiritually strong; the last step is completed when we fully believe we have gained the strength of courage. I've often constructed an interior drama or conversation to help me solve a problem or reach a difficult goal. While daydreaming, I've discovered, again and again, new and surprising ways to act in a strong, God-centered manner.

The second exercise, recording and exploring our dreams, refers to the questioning process we follow when we search for meaning to our dreams. I've found it helpful to record my dreams in as much detail as possible, so that I can try to discover any significant patterns repeated over time. Next I try to make connections between the dream and events in my daily life. I usually ask myself if there is any association between what happened in my dream and stressful situations and problems in my life. Repeatedly, such a process has led me toward greater awareness and insight into my beliefs, feelings, and actions. For those who wish to delve more thoroughly into the dream realm, I would strongly recommend working with a qualified Jungian analyst concerned with spiritual growth.

The third exercise, building a lively imagination by practicing one of the arts, makes us full participants in the creative process. Here we take our thoughts and feelings and give them new forms through the movement of dance, through the shape of clay or stone, in the brush stroke or piano chord, in poem or in song. Creating these forms, we can gain a different perspective and increased understanding of our mental processes.

Recently, I taught myself how to play yet another musical instrument, the alto recorder. Simple to learn and easy to carry with me wherever I go, the recorder allows me to create music at the oddest hours and in the most unlikely settings. Whether it be in a secluded corner of an airport terminal or along a deserted stretch of the Roanoke River where I frequently walk when I'm home, I have found playing the recorder a way of unlocking a new source of creative power within me. It is a power that strengthens me in my determination to relate better to God, self, and others. I suspect that such a source of creative power is readily available to each of us, if only we are willing to tap it.

In his letter to the members of the Roman church, the apostle Paul admonished them not to conform to the evil patterns of this world, "but be transformed by the renewing of your mind" (Rom. 12:2). Daydreaming, dream exploration, and developing a lively imagination are three specific ways in which we can harness our curiosity to renew our minds and transform weakness into strength.

Wisdom

The second creative quality we wish to develop is wisdom. By wisdom, I mean more than the accumulation of knowledge gained by the five senses and reason. For me, wisdom also includes all we have gained by our experiences within the spiritual domain that we then put into Christlike practice.

When we break down this rather daunting definition, the quality of wisdom becomes relatively simple to understand. It consists of what we know and have experienced. It also assumes that we will use all we have learned in a way that personifies the revealed character and will of God.

Wisdom becomes both the accumulation and the reflection of what we know to be true, including our own powerlessness and God's supreme power in our lives and in the world. Accepting our weakness, we prepare ourselves to become spiritually strong. And to gain such strength, which is one aspect of the revealed character of God, we need to develop wisdom. Meditation, devotional reading, silent and verbal prayer, individual Bible study, God-centered conversation, and group discipleship courses continue to be the best avenues to follow in gaining wisdom.

Yet here we run into another paradox in the spiritual life. Something we can work for, wisdom also is a divine gift. Although the first nine chapters of the Book of Proverbs urge us to seek wisdom, we can't hope to receive this gift until we both revere God and obey the Word of God. We find these two conditions stated clearly in the Scriptures, starting with the psalmist's declaration that "The fear of the Lord is the beginning of wisdom" (Ps. 111:10) and ending with Paul's reminder to Timothy that "from infancy you have known the holy Scriptures, which are able to make you wise for salvation through faith in Christ Jesus" (2 Tim. 3:15).

When we stand in awe of God's holiness and spend sufficient time studying the Word, we prepare our spirits to receive that from God, which can make us wise. We also are ready to put our knowledge into practice by applying what we've learned to the daily living of our lives.

We soon confront the difficult task of stripping away illusion and false sentiment. I'll be the first to admit that I don't understand the God who controls creation, nor am I able to discern divine purpose in the providential course of events. Only when I've become realistic about who and what I am in relation to a powerful, inscrutable, yet loving God, do I move away from ignorant illusions or sentimentality.

Besides practicing this new realism, we develop wisdom by working hard and joyfully at whatever we're called to do. The only way I've succeeded in doing this is when I live fully in the present moment and use what good sense and talents I've been granted.

In *Knowing God,* J. I. Packer summarized well the creative practice of wisdom when he wrote,

Thus the effect of His gift of wisdom is to make us more humble, more joyful, more godly, more quick-sighted as to His will, more resolute in the doing of it and less troubled (not less sensitive, but less bewildered) than we were at the dark and painful things of which our life in this fallen world is full.[1]

Practicing wisdom, we are strengthened by the deepening of our relationship with God and its creative expression in our own lives and in the lives of those we meet. And when all our relationships reflect this central one, we bring to them the last creative quality associated with the strength of courage. We bring a joy that arises naturally from the wisdom now flourishing within us.

Joy

The third creative quality that helps us develop the strength of courage is joy. Too often we equate joy with happiness, when satisfaction is actually closer to the biblical meaning of joy. As a fruit of the Spirit, joy can be defined as that deep, inner satisfaction we feel when we depend on the Spirit for the power to live a Christlike life. At the same time, joy is also that satisfaction we feel when we take responsibility to show, by our actions, the workings of the Spirit in our lives.

I have found that joy doesn't come from those things of the world that give me happiness, no matter how pleasurable they may be. The source of my joy can be found, instead, in my relationship with the divine. When I'm obedient to God's will, I know a quiet exhilaration that surpasses any happiness rooted in the temporal.

We each experience the strongest creative joy when we follow our Lord's leading. Even in the midst of our suffering, however, we come to know a sense of satisfaction arising out of our faithfulness. We feel no pleasure in our suffering or that of others, no satisfaction in our pain or the evil that makes us fearful. Instead, we feel thankful that we're growing toward courage through this suffering while experiencing the healing presence of our God.

From such thanksgiving springs the strength of obedient joy. We look beyond our powerlessness, beyond evil fear, and beyond suffering to fix our sights on the eternal. Dante wrote that sorrow remarries us to God. When we renew our commitment to God, we begin to feel a divine healing love, which strengthens all our relationships, our spirits, and our lives.

We then are capable of following Nehemiah's injunction to the returned exiles: "Don't grieve, for the joy of the Lord is your strength" (Neh. 8:10). We try to accept our pain, grief, and loss by focusing on our growing commitment to live for and by Something infinitely higher than ourselves. And that Something, the Triune God of the Old and New Testament, shares joy with us, the created, in proportion to our obedience to the divine will.

If obedience is the key to discovering joy, confessing our sins numbers among the most creative ways we can experience joy. Sin separates us from God: through confession, that break is healed. When we recognize that we have sinned, admit it before God, and ask God's forgiveness, we know the joy that comes from having our relationship with the divine restored.

Our trust in the healing power of the Lord increases, making our act of confession more strengthening to the spirit than any sermon delivered. We have admitted our weakness, confessed in spite of our fear, and been forgiven by a loving God. We now experience joy at our restoration, joy over our salvation, joy for the presence of God.

I can only imagine David's agony after choosing to commit both adultery with Bathsheba and murder in order to marry her. When he prayed for forgiveness, he asked specifically that the Lord restore to him "the *joy* of your salvation" (Ps 51:12). And when he confessed and felt God's forgiving love, David cried, "Rejoice in the Lord and be glad, you righteous; sing, all you who are upright in heart!" (Ps. 32:11).

David, the forgiven, rejoicing psalmist, also shows us a second creative way we may exercise the quality of joy. So many passages of his songs bubble over with the delightful, laughing, music-making revelry of good humor, which numbers high among God's great gifts to us. Time and again, David exhorts us to clap our hands and sing joyfully, to skillfully play the harp and lyre, to shout for joy, to be filled with laughter, to praise with joyous song, music, smiles, and shouts. For him, having a right relationship with God was cause for joyous celebration, even for dancing before the Lord with all his might. He had no use for bored, gloomy, complaining, glum religious attitudes or responses.

We would do well to follow David's joyful example. Developing a balanced, mature sense of humor that appropriately displays our inner joy saves us from the snares of self-pity, self-importance, and false pride. While I'm singing a heartfelt, joyful song of praise to God or smiling with honest good cheer in the face of adversity, I am able to shift my perspective from the limited constricting one of self to the glory and wonder of God. Grounded in the joyous reality of the present moment, genuine humor strengthens me to live faithful to Christ during the pain-filled moments of my life.

The Strength of Courage

The creative expression of curiosity, wisdom, and joy enables us to see through the evil fear of our powerlessness to Someone beyond, in whose image and likeness we wish to be changed. In developing the strength of courage, we show our willingness to be used as we grow in the character of God.

The strength of courage then becomes one more step in our progression toward restoring the lost likeness of Christ, whose life exemplifies the wholeness of courage.

The strength aspect of courage is perhaps best defined as that firmness of mind and will to act in a Christlike manner *in spite of* our fear of being powerless. We have actively prepared ourselves and sought to be transformed from spiritual weakness to strength by living the central lesson of the Cross. We understand the need for and embrace sacrifice and surrender, suffering and dying to all those aspects of self that stand between God and us. Although we cannot understand God's purpose in most human suffering and tragedies, we admit to our powerlessness by surrendering every aspect of our lives to God's control.

We know fear even as we experience the transformation that cleanses evil and empowers us to change from fearful to courageously strong in Christ. Emerging from this spiritual place of change, we take on the responsibility of renewing those creative qualities of curiosity, wisdom, and joy, which draw us closer to the strength of God. Our strength doesn't come from any physical capacity but from a human will that is obedient to the divine will. Obedience to God becomes the basis from which our indomitable courage is released. From there flows the power to be strong.

Practicing the Strength of Courage

The early morning air held the delightful promise of a typical Jerusalem spring day. Yet the woman who carried burial spices and perfumes through the cemetery garden in the predawn darkness felt only the crushing burden of her own sorrow and loss. The man who had cast our her seven demons, the man who had forgiven, taught, and healed her and countless others during his three-year ministry in Galilee and Judea, the man who had been hailed as the Messiah on the streets of Jerusalem only one week earlier, now was dead. Most heartbreaking of all, Jesus of Nazareth had been put to death as a common criminal, nailed to a cross at Golgotha between two thieves. Tortured, mocked, deserted by his followers, and scorned, Jesus had suffered horribly until released from pain by death. A handful of disciples had found the spiritual strength of courage to remain at the foot of the cross, to take possession of the dead body, hastily wrap it, and place it within the rock tomb in the garden. Joseph of Arimathea, a member of the ruling Sanhedrin, had shown even greater courage. He had taken official responsibility for the body of a crucified criminal to be placed in his tomb in the private cemetery garden.

But on this spring morning Mary of Magdala approached the tomb only with women disciples. Despite their shock and grief, they wanted to anoint Jesus' body properly, finishing the burial preparations interrupted by the Sabbath. If they felt fear, their actions didn't show it. At the first opportunity—dawn of the day after the Sabbath—they left the place where the devastated remnant of Jesus' followers remained hidden, and publicly approached a tomb sealed and guarded by the Jewish authorities on Pilate's orders. In coming to the cemetery, these women acted out a statement of faith expressing their continued belief in and love for the One they called Teacher and Master.

Although gospel accounts differ as to what happened when the women reached the empty tomb, certain consistencies emerge from the stories: Mary Magdalene was definitely present; beings from the spiritual domain were present, urging Mary not to be afraid, for the Lord had risen from the dead; Jesus appeared to Mary, again urging her to feel no fear and to share the joyous news with his disciples. We can only imagine Mary Magdalene's feelings—her possible hesitation, her rational disbelief fighting with her spiritual sureness that Jesus, indeed, had done the impossible, her growing excitement, her elation and tears of thanksgiving and joy.

No matter exactly how the events in the cemetery garden unfolded, we know from these four accounts that Mary of

Magdala was honored as no other woman or man in history has been honored. She was chosen as the first to see, to touch, and to speak with Jesus after the resurrection. She was also chosen to proclaim the incredible fact of the Risen Christ, a divine command that could only be followed with great strength of courage.

The gospels state that Mary Magdalene felt great fear in coming face to face with the overwhelming reality of the spiritual realm. Angels, mysterious bolts of lightning, rolled-back boulders, and missing bodies would cause the strongest among us to feel fainthearted. But when Mary encountered Jesus' transformed presence, she gained a strength that grew out of her earlier, unshakable confidence of courage in God the Father and Son.

She knew the confidence of courage because she believed. She knew the strength of courage because she experienced the transforming power of Christ's presence, a power that had conquered evil, suffering, and death. And she practiced the strength of courage when she obeyed Jesus' command and announced to the fear-ridden disciples, "I have seen the Lord!"

Mary may have sensed that these men, hiding in terror from the Jews who had killed their leader, wouldn't believe her story about an empty tomb, two supernatural beings in brilliant raiment, and a conversation with the Risen Christ. Although the disciples knew the depths of her grief and felt her sorrow and pain, they most likely would attribute such a tale to feminine hysteria or overwrought emotions. But practicing the strength of courage, Mary Magdalene rushed to tell them about the resurrection, despite the expected reaction.

In obedience to the Teacher they all had loved, Mary shared with the disciples her joyous discovery that Jesus was alive. Her priorities were in order. She believed, obeyed, and shared her experiential knowledge of Jesus. She knew Who was in control, empowering her to be neither apologetic nor aggressive in giving the disciples the Lord's message.

Mary's strength of courage was gentle rather than harsh, firm rather than rigid, open and uninhibited rather than hidden and reserved. We, too, must learn to practice such open, gentle might. Admitting that the Lord's power, not ours, is alive and working within us, we embody spiritual power through our submission. Knowing that the strength of courage grows out of our relationship with the divine, we allow ourselves to be used by God. In spite of our human weakness and fear, we let ourselves become instruments for growth and change while actively increasing our curiosity, wisdom, and joy for human good and divine glory.

Experiencing the confidence and the strength of courage, we release ourselves from the tyranny of fear formerly governing our lives. Practicing these two cornerstones of courage, we are ready to build on both our confidence and our strength to meet the third challenge in overcoming fear and developing authentic courage.

We've looked inward to create spiritual assurance and gentle might. Now we will look beyond ourselves to the ways our broken fellowship with God and others are reflected in our hostile and fractured world. There we find the genuinely evil twin fears of commitment and rejection present, contributing to the profound sense of alienation pervading our relationships with God, with one another, and with our environment. Selfishness lies at the heart of this isolation, a selfishness that nurtures evil and rejects Jesus' call to servanthood.

In the third challenge, we will discover how to progress from selfishness to compassionate service, from our fear of commitment and rejection to caring, which is the third cornerstone of courage. Reaching out to others with this caring of courage, we will approach the healing of creation and the wholeness of God's kingdom.

III. THE THIRD CHALLENGE
Moving from Selfishness to Caring

Even in darkness light dawns for the
upright,
for the gracious and compassionate
and righteous.

(PS. 112:4)

7. Isolation

Early this morning I awoke to the incessant ringing of the phone. It proved to be a foretaste of what lay ahead during the remaining morning hours. Friends and relatives scattered across the country who had received copies of my latest book called with words of encouragement and congratulations. Strangers who had read interviews in eastern North Carolina papers called to welcome me to this new area I now consider home. Since I had recently returned to giving workshops and lectures, I also received requests this morning to participate in conferences some ten and eleven months away.

Let me assure you such a morning is most atypical for me. Since my children are now grown and have left home, my writing days are spent in solitude, my only companions two loving dogs. To work in such isolation is a necessity that I willingly embrace, knowing that, with a telephone call or a short walk down the street, I can spend a few moments deepening a relationship with one of several newfound friends.

Yet only a few months ago a choice between isolation and sharing didn't exist. On moving to our new town, my husband and I lived in a motel for nearly eight weeks. During that time, he immersed himself in his new job, which has a high public profile. Uprooted, lonely, grieving, and scared, I turned those weeks into ones of frantic productivity, including writing the first part of this book.

Although warmly introduced to the community, I kept people at arm's length. With a cynicism born of fear, I shrugged off their friendly advances as superficial remnants of a mythical Southern hospitality. Locked in a motel room writing, I was creating a self-constructed prison that would protect me from the hurt that is an intrinsic part of involvement. If I didn't establish committed relationships with individuals or within the church and community, I reasoned, then I need never fear the pain of loss, separation, or even rejection.

What I hadn't figured into this eminently logical equation were two factors operating beyond the destructive barriers of self. The first was the insistent nudging of the Spirit to advance rather than retreat from truly living a life fully grounded in the divine. That still small Voice within soon grew into an angry roar as I allowed this evil fear of involvement to govern my actions. The second unexpected factor was the unselfish character of many of the people I began to meet in this part of "Down East" North Carolina. They refused to be shut out of my life.

With a persistence that rivaled that of the Holy Spirit, they gently helped me remove the barricades of fear behind which I hid. When I became sick enough to warrant hospitalization, these people quietly delivered home-cooked meals and gallons of nourishing soup. When my car broke down, they provided transportation before I could even summon the nerve to ask. When I was late meeting a deadline, both a typist and proofreader appeared on my doorstep, asking nothing more than sincere thanks for their work.

Only this morning I experienced this privilege of receiving once again. As the phone continued interrupting my writing and my frustration grew, a friend arrived to drive me to her retreat out in the countryside. She also extended an invitation to use it whenever needed. With rare sensitivity, she had guessed at my unspoken longing for a special place of solitude that our charming older home right in the middle of town cannot provide.

In a hostile and broken world reflecting our fractured fellowship with God, one another, and self, such unheralded acts of unselfish compassion remind us that courage, to become the basis of a truly contemporary spirituality, must move beyond learning and living the confidence and strength of courage. Authentic courage demands that we practice the caring of courage. To strive toward wholeness and union with God, we are called to action. Realizing that inner renewal is essential in the first two movements toward courage, we continue our journey by looking outward and becoming engaged in a world created by and largely alienated from God.

In this third challenge to grow in courage, we must move from isolation to compassion, simultaneously turning away from the evil selfishness in our lives while turning toward service to humanity. But before we can embrace the unselfish servanthood from which the caring of courage develops, we first must tear down the bars keeping us in a solitary confinement of the mind, heart, and soul. And to escape from this self-created prison, we begin by exploring the ways in which humanity and the world have become a cracked mirror imperfectly reflecting the Creator.

The Cracked Mirror

It takes little imagination to discover that we, indeed, are a broken people living in a broken world. At this moment, on the classical music station that I listen to when I write, the BBC newscaster is announcing the current trouble spots around the globe. Bombings, riots, massacres, guerilla attacks, outlawed biological warfare, militaristic threats and political posturing, counterthreats and increased posturing only begin the list. Shadowy government policies, elaborate fraudulent schemes, evasions, lies, and irresponsible, uncaring corporate actions are quickly detailed before moving to less global information. By the time the announcer finishes reading those outstanding individual acts of cruelty considered newsworthy and adds a poignant personal piece about grieving relatives of the most recent victims of violence, no doubt is left in my mind that in this life "now we see but a poor reflection as in a mirror" (1 Cor. 13:12).

When the apostle Paul used this image in his letter to the Corinthians, he knew that they would immediately understand what he meant. Corinth was well known for making mirrors of highly polished metal. Since it would be another twelve centuries before the modern mirror was developed, the Corinthian mirror of Paul's day could do no better than give an imperfect reflection of a people and world created by the Almighty. Paul was comfortable with seeing only dimly the Creator whose handiwork we and the world are. He accepted that the finite can never grasp or accurately reflect the infinite.

Over the centuries, we have made tremendous technological advances. Now we can produce not only accurate mirror images but also the weapons that can annihilate God's earthly creations, including the planet itself. Yet we remain poor reflectors of the Almighty.

The One in whose image we are made has not become any less perfect. But we, the created, have become tarnished and cracked as we and the world we tend progress. In this century alone, there have been long moments when we haven't reflected even the vaguest outline of God. Such moments include but are not limited to when we give booby-trapped toys to Afghan children, accept the hate-filled rhetoric of U.S. white supremacist groups, allow the wholesale slaughter of land and sea creatures, and ignore the genocide of ethnic, racial, religious, political, and cultural groups that has taken place on every continent of the world.

God's image hasn't receded from our grasp. We've let our relationship with the Almighty slip away. As we have grown more distant from our Creator, the cracks in the mirror have lengthened. They accurately reflect our break with God, our break with self, and our break with one another. Far removed from the luminous clarity of wholeness, we have become shards exhibiting our severance from all things divine.

What lies at the base of such brokenness? Why do we find it acceptable and even normal to live lives filled with pain in a hostile and fractured world? Why do we cut ourselves adrift from the moorings of a genuinely loving relationship with God, self, and others?

When we look into the cracked mirror of our heart, we have difficulty finding God, wholeness, and fellowship. Instead, isolated people acting with utmost selfishness stare back at us. We see women and men who have chosen to live in a self-made prison of fear rather than walk freely along the arduous, Christlike path of courage.

Isolation and Fear

Our fear of involvement is the foundation on which selfish isolation is built. When we set up boundaries that stop us from developing loving relationships, we are expressing our profound fear of committing our lives wholly to Another and our equally deep fear of committing ourselves to those whose lives we touch.

The evilness of selfish isolation has been enacted on our world stage from the beginning of recorded history. Each time it has made an appearance, four outgrowths of our fear of divine and human involvement emerge. We become *hating, prideful, pretentious, competitive* people rather than living expressions of love, selflessness, honesty, and cooperation.

Recently, I've immersed myself in the chilling literature of the Holocaust, seeking to better understand this well-documented twentieth-century expression of evil. The unvarnished facts defy belief. Those running the efficient Nazi death machine systematically killed over six million men, women, and children, who were deemed unworthy to live due to their race, religion, politics, or ethnicity.

Even more outrageous, those directly responsible for the deaths of the Holocaust victims were aided in their gruesome work by the tacit support, and even approval, of countless others throughout the world. Individually and corporately, as members of civic organizations, religious groups, and political governments, the overwhelming majority of humankind chose to ignore the highly organized slaughter taking place across the face of Europe.

It's obvious that the world's citizens riveted their attention on the more traditional mechanisms of warfare. It's less obvious that these silent others had themselves fallen victim to the fear of involvement. If they had wholly committed themselves to the gospel of love that Jesus Christ revealed in his teachings and life, would they have been able to harbor suspicion of and hatred for those different from themselves? If they had wholeheartedly believed all humanity to be children of God, would they have accepted the false claims of superiority used to justify genocide? Time and again, I found myself wondering what lies, what perverted standards of competition, what selfish pretenses and insidious comparisons they developed so that they could turn away from those who needed their help to exist.

Succumbing to the very real evil of fear—and to the fear of involvement specifically—much of humankind failed to develop the courage to care. Without a commitment to the message of Jesus, they felt little responsibility for those classified different, inferior, and less deserving of life. Lacking involvement in a loving relationship with the divine, they knew none of the selfless compassion that marks a loving human relationship.

Lest we feel complacent because the Holocaust ended over four decades ago, we need only look at the events taking place in our world today to realize that the fear of involvement is alive and flourishing. So is isolation based on selfishness. If the print and broadcast media are to be believed, we are again opting for intimidation over intimacy, conquest over compassion, and greed over giving.

We seem to forget that, first and foremost, we are members of the family of God. Within this unit rooted in the divine, we belong to other, well-defined families, beginning with the personal and ending with the global. Whether by choice or circumstance, we are part of a nuclear, extended, church, work, community, state, national, and international family. Some of these family groups are more important to us than others, but our relationships within each help us define who we are, what we believe, and how we express that identification and live those beliefs.

When we allow the fear of involvement to govern our lives, we withdraw from active participation in the family of God. With the holy and the human, we exhibit traits expressing the evil of selfishness rather than the selflessness of God. We put the false idols of avarice, self-interest, and indifference toward others in place of the God of generosity, service, and authentic caring.

Too often, we fail to see the ripple effect of our acts of selfishness as they filter through the different family groups to which we belong. Cheating on our income tax, using phosphates to clean our clothes, turning away a relative in need of emotional support, allowing a racial slur to go unchallenged, failing to meet a financial pledge, cutting corners in a presentation, venting our frustration on an innocent bystander, abusing our natural resources, refusing to share our "hard-worked-for" abundance with the "undeserving" have-nots are just some of the many selfish, isolating choices that we make daily.

Each decision to act selfishly is based on our fear of involvement, and each action extends far beyond the boundaries of self. Paradoxically, by isolating ourselves, we negatively affect so many lives. With each act of selfishness, we cause our tenuous relationship with God and other people to become even more fragile.

Each selfish, isolating choice is a vote against becoming involved with the demands and expectations of God and others. Noninvolvement is safe. We run no danger of disappointing anyone on any level in the family of God. Aware of our isolation, other people soon learn to expect nothing of us.

Fortunately for us, our Lord is not so easily put off. Created by God to grow ever closer to wholeness, we find little peace living fearful lives of selfish isolation. The brilliant Church father, Augustine, in the fourth century, and the brilliant Trappist monk and reformer of monastic life, Thomas Merton, in the twentieth, understood this fact all too well. Both wrote spiritual classics detailing their search for peace—a search that carried them away from selfish pursuits in the temporal world to the selfless expression of eternal realities.

In Saint Augustine's *Confessions* and Merton's *The Seven Storey Mountain*, we read of their passionate struggle to find peace in the love of God rather than in the love of self. As they matured spiritually, these two men from different cultures and centuries walked similar paths of growth. They moved through the pain created by their selfishness to reach the caring of courage that only a selfless love of God brings.

To follow that same pathway requires that we, too, confront our pain. Alone, increasingly cut off from God and other people, we are blinded by the darkness of our selfish isolation. We hurt others, we hurt God, and we hurt ourselves. The only way we can gauge how much the evil fear of involvement has damaged our spirits is to examine the interrelated wounds fear has inflicted and bring them into the healing presence of God.

Insecurity

Our spiritual wounds are not always readily evident. The fear that created these wounds also drives us to keep them hidden from ourselves as well as from others. But no matter how thoroughly we try to disguise or hide them, the pain they cause refuses to go away.

Insecurity is one such spiritual wound that we ultimately cannot ignore. It keeps manifesting itself in our relationships from the personal to the global. Look at our divorce statistics, listen to the topics discussed on talk shows, read the titles of the current self-help bestsellers, count the increasing number of uncommitted relationships, and we see an American population insecure about loving and being loved.

Next take a look at our sagging church attendance, the decrease in volunteer work, the popularity of books, tapes, and seminars on the principles of success, competition, and winning at all costs, and we see an American society filled with people insecure about their standing in the church, workplace, and community.

When we look at the declining number of citizens voting, the increasing lack of political involvement, and the limited protests against unjust or inhumane policies, we see an American public insecure about their impact on any level of government.

Finally, look at the sheer number of nuclear weapons, the percentage of our budget going to defense, government-sanctioned terrorism, and government-subsidized dumping of surplus food while millions starve at home and abroad. What we see is a nationally shared insecurity about our privileged status among people lacking the same economic opportunities and means for social progress.

From the interpersonal to the international, insecurity based on a fear of involvement makes openness, sharing, and vulnerability all but impossible. We doom ourselves to expending our energies defending our borders and hoarding our resources. Protecting our interests, we slam the gates shut on compassion and caring. And the pain caused by our fearful reactions is felt throughout God's family.

Cynicism

Cynicism wounds the human spirit by attempting to eradicate the unique dignity and worth of God's creation. When we fear involvement, one way we counter that fear is by accepting selfishness as the governing factor in our conduct. Overtly holding such a view, we no longer believe in other people's honesty, sincerity, ethical and moral attitudes or actions. Nor do we see them as children of a divine Creator.

Our cynical feelings toward our fellow human beings range from distrustful doubt to contemptuous and mocking disbelief. Convinced that every person is motivated wholly by self-interest, the cynic expects nothing but the worst in human conduct. Pessimism replaces hope, isolation replaces intimacy, sarcasm replaces joy, and the self replaces God in the cynic's life.

Cynicism is insidious. Rejecting God and others happens so gradually that we barely notice it until the change is almost complete. And much like the related spiritual wound of insecurity, cynicism has global as well as personal ramifications.

A young woman, whom I had helped raise during the early years of my marriage, called late one January night, her voice slurred by a near-lethal combination of brandy and Valium. Her twenty-two years had been pain-filled ones, beginning with abuse by her natural mother and culminating in rejection by her most recent lover. The years in between had been lived with utmost caution. When she came to stay with me, she dared not hope for happiness. When touched, she would stiffen, expecting a blow to follow. Possessing a sharp mind and delightfully dry wit, she kept both under careful control.

Slowly, even these few positive qualities began to change. The dry wit became acidic; the inquisitive mind, fault-finding. Early on, she had equated involvement with pain. Fearful and suspicious of love, she never stopped retreating from others until all she had left was the utter safety—and emptiness—of an isolated self.

On that January night of her first suicide attempt, she had tried to numb the pain of her wholly selfish existence. She also had enough self-interest left to cry for the help she so desperately needed. Confronting and solving her problems was a long, painful process, which she courageously suffered along with setbacks and moments of avoidance. During those difficult years of counseling, she also gained an advanced degree in clinical psychology. Today, involved in fighting the epidemic of teenage suicides in this country, she works with adolescents in a family crisis center. Few traces of cynicism remain. She willingly accepts the risks of involvement, letting the selfless giving of Christ guide her.

Depression

The third wound we experience is a familiar one. A literal pressing down or lowering of body, mind, and spirit, depression is frequently referred to as the common cold of the modern psyche. When we break our contact with God and others, our capacity to feel and respond becomes diminished. When we avoid the risks of involvement, we soon discover that life has grown achingly empty of the meaningful joy of communion with God and one another.

We know true darkness when we allow fear to lower us into depression. In the intolerable isolation we experience, we abandon ourselves to that darkness. Expecting nothing from ourselves, we expect nothing from God or humanity. Having discarded caring for ourselves, we soon lose the ability to care for others.

Only in the most recent literature of depression are therapists beginning to explore the importance of spiritual beliefs in the treatment of depressive conditions. They are recognizing that for mental, physical, and spiritual health, we, the created, need to mirror our Creator accurately. When we perceive ourselves as uncaring in an equally selfish world, our vision is an evil distortion of a loving, empathetic God. Lost in our separateness, we know a suffocating loneliness born of evil and fear. With the psalmist, we pray aloud from the painful depths of our depression,

> My soul is full of trouble
>   and my life draws near the grave,
> I am counted among those who go down to the pit;
>   I am like a man without strength.
> I am set apart with the dead,
>   like the slain who lie in the grave,
> whom you remember no more,
>   who are cut off from your care. . . .
>   the darkness is my closest friend.
>
> (PS. 88:4–5,18)

The evil fear of involvement does have the power to destroy us by inflicting deep spiritual wounds. But insecurity, cynicism, and depression need not be fatal to spiritual growth. There is an alternative to the darkness that permits no reflection of God to enter our souls. We begin by letting the Light become our closest friend.

My exuberant Italian grandfather, who as a young man lived in Rome, used to call his favorite saints "Children of the Light." From the time I was very young, Poppy would share, in typical dramatic fashion, his love for these men and women with a spellbound audience of adoring grandchildren.

One story I remember vividly was about a monk named Telemachus. An old man, he had spent many years living as a hermit in the desert until the day God told him to go to Rome. A little confused but obedient, Telemachus made the long journey to the city, arriving there during the Roman victory celebration over the Gauls. Hesitantly, he followed the noisy crowds into the Colosseum and watched the spectacle unfold. As gladiators fought one another and wild beasts to a bloody death, the good *abba* was horrified by what he saw. Horrified and no longer confused. He knew why God had led him to Rome.

Despite his age and tired body, Telemachus leapt over the wall separating the bleachers from the arena and stood in the center of the Colosseum. "Stop," he called out. "In the name of Jesus Christ, stop."

The Colosseum grew silent. The gladiator nearest the monk struck him with the flat side of his sword. Telemachus went sprawling in the blood-stained dirt. Pulling himself up, the monk cried out again, "In the name of Jesus Christ, stop."

The crowd grew angry at having their entertainment interrupted by this crazy old monk. Shouts of "Kill him!" could be heard. A willing gladiator stepped forward and ran a sword through Telemachus's body. The monk crumpled to the ground, dead.

This happened in a city of people who had been taught the

gospel of Christ. But they existed in the fearful darkness of selfish isolation, their lives untouched by the care and compassion of Jesus. When Telemachus fell dead, an unexpected silence filled the stadium. Singly, and in small groups, people began to leave the Colosseum. Soon it was empty.

Although crowds filled the stands in the years to come, gladiator games were never held again. Telemachus, the old desert monk, had become a beacon of light in the darkness of early Christian Rome. With his life, he taught these Romans the care and compassion of Christ. And they learned the lesson well enough to demand an end to their games of slaughter.

We, too, can become reflections of the divine Light rather than mirror the evil darkness of fear. When, at last, we can see ourselves for what we truly are—broken people in need of healing, vulnerable people in need of caring, fearful people in need of giving—we are ready to replace a life of selfishness with one of service. Only in this way we can teach ourselves and others the caring of courage.

8. Service

You are driving along a two-lane road early one rainy evening. Dressed for a special occasion, you're anxious about arriving on time, about your appearance, about how you'll interact with the other guests invited to this dinner party. Suddenly an approaching station wagon skids on the wet highway surface, spins out of control, and lands in a ditch on the other side of the road.

It's taken only a few seconds to happen. Aware of the line of cars behind you, you hesitate to hit your brakes and pull to the side. You may cause an accident, you rationalize. People on the other side of the road will find it safer to stop and offer help, you continue to reason as the seconds tick by. You fail to mention to yourself that, in this driving rainstorm, your hair and clothing will be ruined if you leave your car to help. Neither do you admit that if there are injured people, you'd be placing yourself in a potentially risky position with a litigation-happy public. And if police reports become necessary, you may as well forget about the dinner altogether.

Do you continue driving to your party or turn around to help the people in the station wagon?

Let us take another situation that can occur in the course of a typical day in late-twentieth-century America. You've joined a group of friends for an informal get-together after work. The talk meanders from the latest political scandal to the effects of the recent hot weather on your backyard gardens. Suddenly, someone repeats a particularly vicious rumor about an unpopular manager at work, a man who recently caused one friend to lose his job and forced another into early retirement. You know the rumor to be untrue, yet you hesitate setting the record straight. Your resentment over his shoddy and unjust treatment of your co-workers stands in your way.

Do you speak up on his behalf or let the conversation continue uninterrupted?

A self-centered family member, who appears to thrive on creating dissension, arrives for a weekend visit. She and her husband spend the first few hours flaunting their affluent lifestyle and belittling the values of simplicity, community service, and active church participation that you hold dear. As the day drags on, you find yourself reaching the limits of your tolerance. Feeling you're incapable of responding to another snide comment with anything approaching generosity of spirit, you withdraw into an angry silence. When she does notice the change in your behavior, she asks you what is wrong.

Do you respond with continued silence, biting anger, or gentle confrontation?

You and your spouse have faced a difficult financial year together. You both have sacrificed to meet your obligations honorably. For the first time in months, there's money left over to spend on something other than necessities. In your imagination, you've enjoyed spending it half a dozen times over.

That very afternoon, a cold, overbearing acquaintance visits with a disturbing request. She is working to maintain a battered women's shelter and firmly states that today she doesn't need pledges of time, clothing, or household goods—pledges that you filled in the past and never received thanks for. She wants money. An emergency situation exists. The lease on the shelter will be lost if she doesn't raise more money today.

You and your spouse exchange cautious looks. You've struggled so long with few rewards. You've discussed at length which book, which cassette, which pair of sandals you wanted to buy. You read uncertainty, disappointment, and confusion in each other's eyes. You ponder your options. You could offer this woman all, your half, or even a portion of your half of the money you've managed to save. Or you could refuse this pushy acquaintance's request. She's never appreciated your efforts anyway.

What do you choose to give?

Every day we make choices that center on our fear of involvement. We decide daily how much we are willing to risk in giving of ourselves to others. We know that to become involved is to open ourselves to the demands of painful sacrifice. Yet as we have learned, to remain outside a loving relationship with God, self, or others is to embrace certain destruction of the spirit.

Our choices grow increasingly clear. We may allow our fear of involvement to cripple or kill any hope of living life in the spirit. Or we may take the one route open to those seeking to overcome the evil arising from the fear of involvement. Jesus described this path to his chosen disciples when he told them, "Whoever wants to become great among you must be your servant, and whoever wants to be first must be slave of all. For even the Son of Man did not come to be served, but to serve, and to give his life as a ransom for many" (Mark 10:43–45).

If we are to replace our fear of involvement with the caring of courage, we must begin by engaging in a life of service characterized by authentic selflessness. Jesus Christ pointed us toward this pathway of service with his words and with his life. In God's Son, we have the perfect model of servant-hood. Through Jesus' teachings and the events of his brief life, we discover a man who wasn't afraid to suffer the consequences of becoming involved. He showed us how to give unselfishly of all that we are and have; he also taught us how to serve unselfishly all whom we meet.

To follow in Jesus' footsteps along this pathway leading to courage, we must redirect our focus from the rewards of serving to the redemptive aspects of service itself. Unselfish, Christlike servanthood is more than doing good to and for others, more than social work, community action, or social reform. Alleviating human misery is a worthy goal, yet selfless service requires that we also become "a fellow workman with God," as the Dominican philosopher Meister Eckhart taught seven centuries ago. To be God's worker, we must learn to share our lives, our fears, and our selfless visions with others in the same redemptive spirit that Jesus shared his life with us. Following Christ's lead, we must give and serve with no selfish end product in sight. We seek only to bring God into others' lives and to bring others to God.

Mother Teresa of Calcutta is one of God's outstanding workers in a world where authentic servanthood is practiced by few and mastered by even fewer. Much has been written and said about this humble Apostle of the Unwanted and her life of Christian love and service. We know somewhat less about the Missionaries of Charity, which Mother Teresa founded. A religious order dedicated to serving the poorest of the poor, the Missionary Sisters and Brothers work on every continent fulfilling their vow to God to give "wholehearted free service to the poor."

Yet, it is the International Association of Co-workers of Mother Teresa that holds my greatest interest. This worldwide organization, affiliated with the Missionaries of Charity, consists of people of all ages, nationalities, and religions. Their goal is deceptively simple: to unite in prayer and sacrifice to help people recognize God in the person of the poor and love God better through works of charity and service to the poor.

Like the Missionary Brothers and Sisters, and Mother Teresa herself, the Co-workers are people from ordinary backgrounds committed to an extraordinary way of life. They express their love of God by being sensitive and responsive to the needs of the poor, particularly those who are unwanted and unloved. Carrying these words of Christ in their hearts, the Co-workers have made them the basis of their actions:

For I was hungry and you gave me something to eat, I was thirsty and you gave me something to drink, I was a stranger and you invited me in, I needed clothes and you clothed me, I was sick and you looked after me, I was in prison and you came to visit me. . . . whatever you did for one of the least of these brothers of mine, you did for me.

(Matt. 25:25–35, 40)

Mother Teresa's Co-workers exercise voluntary poverty and sacrifice luxuries, conducting their home and business lives with economy and austerity. They donate to the Missionaries of Charity whatever time and material help they are able to provide. While living with their families and working in jobs beyond the framework of the religious order, the Co-workers serve others with their prayers, time, money, and individual acts of sacrifice and giving.

To me, the Co-workers of Mother Teresa embody servant-hood on a scale readily attainable for those of us who haven't been called to a vocation within a religious order. They guide us along the spiritual path of growth as we struggle to trans-form our devastating fear of involvement into a genuine caring rooted in courage. Redirecting our lives to conform to Jesus' mandate that we become servant and slave to all, we look to the Co-workers of Mother Teresa to learn the art of unselfish living.

Respect

To serve rather than be served, the first quality we need to develop is respect. Until we can recognize the dignity, the individuality, and the infinite value of every human life, we will fail to grow from fear, through service, to courage.

When we see the homeless sleeping on heating grates in our nation's capital, do we, in our hearts, see them as children of God with as much right to the things of life, love, and service as anybody else? What about the mentally ill? The economically deprived who have no skills with which to compete? The destitute, institutionalized elderly? The wretchedly ill inhabiting the slums of every city? The starving nomads trekking across the wastelands and battlefields of the world?

We already know what the correct spiritual answer to these questions should be. Only in the recesses of our own hearts can we discover whether we truly believe in the dignity of *every* person and the sacredness of *all* life. Without a respect for all others based on their sacred worth as God's children, we can't hope to become God's fellow workers in service. Without such respect, we're incapable of relating to that of God existing within each one of us.

When we gain respect imbued with sacredness, we greet God with a smile everywhere we go and in everyone we meet. With such respect, we find Christ hidden in the homeless of our city streets, in the mentally and physically ill, in the deprived, institutionalized and starving masses shunted aside and ignored by those people who are dominated by selfishness and fear.

I remember once reading that the Lutheran pastor and martyr Dietrich Bonhoeffer corrected someone for speaking about "the Christian life." Bonhoeffer felt the man should have said "the Christ living in us" instead. Seeking to learn respect, we find this distinction important, but it doesn't go far enough. We are acknowledging that Christ dwells in our own hearts and in the hearts of his followers. Yet it is imperative that we also recognize God in all people and that we help others to recognize this spiritual reality dwelling among us.

We easily respect those we admire and love. When we are capable of giving respect naturally to the materially, socially, and spiritually deprived, we are ready to learn how to practice the second quality of servanthood in our lives.

Responsibility

Obeying the repeated scriptural command to serve requires us to become responsible. Most often we think of responsibility in philosophical terms having to do with fulfilling a duty, exercising a privilege, or being accountable for a behavior. Yet developing the responsible attitudes and actions of a servant has little to do with philosophy and much to do with deepening our relationship with God. Only by turning inward to discover the revealed God within, can we then turn outward to act in accordance with our discovery. By directly and immediately experiencing the wholeness of God, we become empowered to return to a broken world as workers in God's service.

The Latin root word *respondēre* reveals that authentic servanthood in God's name lies at the heart of responsibility, for it means "to promise" or "to answer in trust." When God calls us to become servants, it is our responsibility to respond to the Deity in terms of those promises of faith we have made, including our pledge of obedience. We have no choice. Our service to God and others is our answer in trust and our promise fulfilled to Christ, who came into this world to serve and expects the same from us.

To serve responsibly in a world dimly reflecting God's image, we need to consider Christ's description of the servant as a light shining before others, accurately reflecting God within and beyond. The image of a servant responsible for shedding light in a shadowy world is one that I have always liked for its directness and simplicity. Light dispels darkness, gives direction, and is a reassuring beacon to the lost.

When friends took me spelunking in a series of caves on the eastern plains of New Mexico a couple of years ago, I learned anew the importance of being a bearer of light in a darkened world. There, sounds can be deceiving, giving no indication of direction while the darkness itself invites both confusion and fear. Responsible spelunkers help most by casting light rather than speeches. Their actions, far more than their words, have the power to guide others out of the frightening caverns of darkness.

As reflections of the Inward Light, we similarly must serve those lost in darkness. Through our actions, not our sermons, we uphold our promise to God to be responsible bearers of the Light.

Sacrifice

Serving also requires sacrifice. As God's fellow workers, we will face difficulties, opposition, and discouragement as we seek to do God's will by helping others. In developing a heart open to the suffering of others, we can expect to meet our share of suffering. Service cannot happen without pain.

Our sacrifice in helping others can take myriad forms. We may experience ridicule or callous disregard by people we once had considered our friends. As our perception of the world changes and we increasingly identify and act on our shared humanity with the poor, the despised, and the dispossessed, we may know an inner confusion matched by social rejection and possibly even ostracism.

Introducing behavior that is contrary to what has always been considered "normal" is risky. When an individual behaves contrary to the expected norm, be it for good or for evil, the universal human response is to attack that person physically or verbally.

Threatened by that which is different, we fear and resist change on the physical, spiritual, and emotional level. As God's fellow workers, we must be ready to be attacked for becoming servants in a world that fears, resists, and rejects servanthood.

I must confess that I've never been fond of the apostle Paul. Although I know he was culture bound, I find that his intolerance, inflexibility, and misogyny stand in the way of my appreciation of his great missionary works and theological brilliance. Yet when he boasted about his sufferings as Christ's servant in his second letter to the church members of Corinth, I realize that Paul catalogued his beatings, stonings, floggings, shipwrecks, and imprisonments in an effort to share with these fledgling Christians what they, too, could expect as authentic servants of Jesus. They—and we—must learn to persevere, despite the suffering that is bound to come our way.

Boldness

No matter what painful experiences we undergo, we must continue to pursue servanthood in a manner reflecting the boldness of Christ. To bear witness against injustice, inhumanity, and other aspects of our brokenness in a darkened world, we need to develop this quality of Christlike boldness in our thoughts and actions.

Boldness has a refreshingly honest and direct simplicity to it. Neither aggressive nor obnoxious, bold servants simply, quietly, and effectively work to alleviate suffering in the most forthright method available. There are no hidden meanings behind their words. There are no half-measures taken either. Boldness is an all-or-nothing phenomenon, for bold servants have grown in their relationships with God enough to take risks in spite of the fear of involvement they feel. Acknowledging the specific ways the Lord wants them to serve, bold disciples of Christ opt for decisive rather than hesitant thoughts, and for daring rather than timid actions.

We begin to be bold servants when we speak freely and openly about how Christ is the ultimate model of servanthood. But too often we stop there. To serve others as Christ has served us, we next need to speak out against the evil practices of the world built on the fear of involvement and then make our actions consistent with our speech. We must dare to go forth and serve others in ways that conflict with their fragmented, fear-filled behavior. Preaching the gospel of service no longer is enough. We must serve others boldly even though we fear it may cost us our friends, our status, our prestige, our families, our financial security, our lives.

Boldness erases the limits we allow fear to place on our ability to serve. With boldness, we not only see but also act from the belief that everyone we meet is our brother and sister in the family of God, deserving of respect, of dignity, of compassion, of giving. With boldness, we place the welfare of others before our own. With boldness, the unwanted and unloved become wanted and loved by us. With boldness, we refuse to hesitate for fear that we may be opposed, we may suffer, we may be rejected, we may offend, we may be in danger.

We have experienced the tyranny of fear and the freedom of sacrifice. Both war within us still. Except now we acknowledge fear's tyranny and refuse to be its slave. Having surrendered ourselves to God, we dare to become Christ's "slave to all" by letting God use us boldly in Christian service.

Generosity of Spirit

Along the border of the United States and Mexico, several *serviglesias,* or serving churches, exist under the auspices of the Presbyterian Border Ministry. In addition to providing a worship center, each *serviglesia* works to meet the particular needs of its community. Prenatal and primary health care programs, consumer education, and small business cooperatives, which provide on-the-job training are only a few of the projects being developed. Nutritionists, bakers, public health nurses, cement-block makers, doctors, economic development specialists, lawyers, cabinet makers, dentists, engineers, carpenters, and teachers volunteer their skills to improve the physical as well as the spiritual life of these communities to which God has called them to serve.

The aptly named *serviglesias* of this border ministry could not grow and flourish without the generosity of spirit of those who give of their time, skills, and money to help their needy neighbors. The fifth quality of servanthood, generosity of spirit, demands of the Christian servant more than impersonal giving. It calls for us to share of ourselves as well as of our possessions or money.

When I think of generosity of spirit, I am reminded of that loyal co-worker of the apostle Paul named Aristarchus. With only five scant comments made about him in the New Testament, we know very little about this Thessalonian, who quietly displayed generosity of spirit. What information we are given is impressive: Aristarchus voluntarily chose to become a slave and give his life over to the work of Christ, no matter where it led him.

We're told that Aristarchus was arrested in Ephesus during the riot following Paul's first appearance there. Becoming Paul's close companion, he journeyed with the apostle from Troas to Jerusalem, and from Jerusalem to Rome before sharing Paul's imprisonment with him. What's less evident in reading the biblical accounts of Aristarchus is the manner in which he accompanied Paul. When the apostle was under arrest and on his way to trial before the Emperor in Rome, Aristarchus had to enroll himself as Paul's slave to be able to stay with him. And tradition has it that Aristarchus, too, died a martyr's death in Rome during Nero's relentless persecution of the Christians.

In spite of this sketchy history of Aristarchus' life as a Christian, we discover certain hallmarks that distinguish those who have developed a generous spirit. They give of themselves; they give willingly; they give in the spirit of self-denial; they give despite earthly loss; they give with obedience to God as the reward. From this first-century Thessalonian to the twentieth-century Missionaries of Charity and their Co-workers, we find that their generosity of spirit is a God-given gift, one that they practiced to benefit others in order to glorify God, not themselves.

As we seek to turn away from the evilness of fear with our acts of service to others, we, too, can become empowered by the Holy Spirit. Receiving the gift of generosity, we learn to serve God best by serving others generously.

All aspects of our lives become a gift to share rather than to possess. Focusing on God, we open our hearts willingly and obediently in service to all our neighbors. And through our selfless words and actions, those we serve can begin to know the glory of the God we love and the generosity of the Son we strive to imitate.

A Religion for Slaves

I began this chapter with four "what-if" scenarios, finishing each with questions about how we might act in that particular situation. In each case, we could choose between being selfish and being caring by responding from a basis of fear or of courage. We either could use the qualities of authentic servanthood to develop a courageous compassion for others or proceed to live in selfish isolation created by fear.

So it is with our lives. We have the freedom to choose between good and evil, between fear and courage, between selfishness and caring. Yet in making evil choices we destroy that very freedom we need most to become selfless, fearless, caring disciples of Christ. "Perfect spiritual freedom is a total inability to make any evil choice," Thomas Merton wrote. "When everything you desire is truly good and every choice not only aspires to that good but attains it, then you are free because you do everything that you want, every act of your will ends in perfect fulfillment."[1]

We are not perfect beings acting always for the good and truly unable to make evil choices. We are imperfect human beings plagued by selfish desires and fear-directed choices. At times, we long for the security of our self-made prisons of isolation. Freedom, and the caring it leads to, frightens us more than any thought of living a painfully selfish existence. And serving others, that necessary step we must take when we choose to become involved, requires us to embrace yet another difficult paradox on our journey toward courage: we can attain spiritual freedom only by becoming servant and slave to all.

Glancing through my journal recently, I was startled by a quotation that fairly leaped off the page at me. "Christianity is a religion for slaves," the French philosopher and mystic

Simone Weil stated. When I copied her words in my journal, I had thought them harshly critical. Since that time, I've learned how affirming they really are.

A religion for slaves is a religion of freedom rather than of fear. To follow Christ along the pathway leading from selfishness to caring, we give up our will for Another's and surrender our self-centered pursuits for God-centered service to others. Despite our ever-present fear of becoming involved, we voluntarily do God's work here and now, in this broken world, with and for our fellow human beings.

Thus enslaved by choice, we truly become free to respect the dignity of others, to be responsible reflections of the Light in their lives, to sacrifice ourselves in alleviating their suffering, to take risks boldly on their behalf, and to share with them on every level of our beings, expecting nothing in return. A Christian slave accurately mirrors the serving Christ, bringing a healing image to a world fragmented by the evilness of fear. It is to this level of slavery and service we aspire. And once immersed in it, we are ready to learn to live the third cornerstone of courage, caring about others with an unselfish and fearless love.

9. Compassion

The first Sunday morning I heard the church bells ringing, I was surprised and delighted. In choosing our present home in a quiet residential section near the center of town, both my husband and I had been pleased to find that it was within easy walking distance of the library, post office, and assorted stores. We also had noticed its central location among the five churches in the area.

It wasn't until that first Sunday morning we discovered just how centrally we were located. The Baptist, Methodist, Presbyterian, First Christian, and Episcopalian churches rang joyful bells, announcing their respective Sunday school classes and early and late morning worship services. That evening, and intermittently throughout the week, other bells continued to interrupt the daily flow of small-town life. With a warm, old-fashioned charm, they could be heard calling townspeople to Bible study classes, young adult groups, choir practices, and discipleship meetings.

Over the months, I've grown fond of these gentle reminders that although we live in this world, we live for Another. Hearing the pealing bells, I tend to think them less an invitation to come to church and more a call to bring Christ's message to the community within hearing range of the bells and beyond. Reminding us of the importance of communal worship, the bells speak to us of communal concerns, too. With their ringing, they hurry our hearts toward devotion and our feet toward putting that devotion into action.

Throughout the centuries, bells have called women and men to worship together in Christ and become engaged in the world outside their church doors as followers of Christ. A shared devotional service and a shared vision of service to others characterized Christianity at its beginning. For the early Christians, faith in Christ and Christlike behavior were integral parts of their distinctively different way of life. As Jim Wallis, in his challenging book *The Call to Conversion*, relates,

They became well known as a caring, sharing, and open community that was especially sensitive to the poor and the outcast. Their love for God, for one another, and for the oppressed was central to their reputation. Their refusal to kill, to recognize racial distinctions, or to bow down before the imperial deities was a matter of public knowledge. [1]

Belief fused with action. Believing in Christ, they became actively involved in the lives of those they encountered. From fellow Christians and outcasts to their Roman and Jewish persecutors, they reached out to serve in Jesus' name.

No matter how noteworthy, service to others, in and of itself, didn't distinguish these early Christians from any other first-century philanthropic group. However, the compassionate quality of their service did. For them, service was a way station along the road from selfishness to caring. They knew their destination was the courageous compassion taught and lived by the Messiah. Believing that Jesus was the Suffering Servant spoken of by the prophet Isaiah, they sought to be like Christ, to become one with those who suffered, and to selflessly alleviate the world's brokenness and pain.

They succeeded admirably. Since then, others have approached that same level of Christian compassion to build bonds rather than boundaries among the family of God. In the last nineteen hundred years, the acts of these compassionate individuals have rung like bells across the centuries, reminding us to continue to seek this Christlike sharing and caring for the spiritual, physical, and emotional welfare of others.

Compassion Lived

During the institutionalized insanity of the Holocaust, an embarrassingly tiny number of individuals risked their lives to protect Jewish men, women, and children. More times than naught, the Jews they helped were strangers to them, yet these individuals disregarded danger, torture, even death, to act with compassion. They defied evil at the risk of their own lives, feeling that to be human is to be caring.

After the war and the birth of the state of Israel, the Israeli government honored over five thousand Gentiles as Hasidei Umot Haolam, the Righteous Among the Nations of the World. To receive this humanitarian honor, each recipient had met three conditions: helped save a Jewish life during the Holocaust; thereby endangering his or her own life; and helped without receiving monetary or other reward. In a powerful book entitled *The Courage to Care,* the stories of some of these rescuers of the Jews are related in their own words and in the words of those they rescued.

On close reading of these documented cases, I was struck, time and again, by certain qualities these compassionate Gentiles shared. They considered themselves to be ordinary people, who wanted to help their neighbors. They said simply that they had no other choice if they were to remain true to God's purpose for them. They said, "I am my brother's keeper"; "I must keep my heart, my hands, my ears open for anybody needy"; "I thought with my heart and then acted"; and "At home and school, our education was directed toward love, compassion, and service to others." These are a small sampling of their quotations that speak of a courageous commitment to unselfish, loving action in a world paralyzed by fear and blinded by selfishness.

From these eloquent stories, we have much to learn about developing the caring of courage in our own lives. To live Christian compassion effectively, we can look to the horrors of the past and in that darkness discover how these few beacons of love and caring shone forth. We can see that although world opinion during the 1930s should have been one of outrage over the atrocities being committed, the large majority of people remained apathetic, uninvolved, unconcerned, and indifferent.

We can also see the chilling effectiveness of the German program, which was accomplished by first isolating Jews and then dividing humankind into opposing groups pitted against one another by age, social class, ethnicity, religion, and nationality.

In such an environment, to develop a heart open to the suffering of others in spite of feeling vulnerable, helpless, and afraid becomes a celebration of love for God in a world ignoring such love. The Righteous Among the Nations of the World saw inhumanity in action and summoned the courage to take risks to replace that evil with love.

There is a Talmudic saying that whoever saves one life, it is as if he or she saved the entire world. In the stories of the Righteous, we are reminded how their actions saved society from being destroyed by its own fear. Taking the responsibility to express their love for God, they acted selflessly to save others. We have much to learn, and our world has much to gain, from their example.

An All-embracing Love

To cast out fear and build a caring society based on a shared biblical vision, we must develop a love strong enough and deep enough to withstand the evil of fear. Loving God is not enough. We are called to love all humanity as fellow members in the family of God. While establishing a caring society, we cannot compromise in terms of love. In helping the defenseless, we must refuse to hate, dehumanize, or hurt the victimizers. Loving God fully, we cannot allow any person to become our enemy.

Countless volumes have been written about this all-embracing love, but nothing matches the clarity of Jesus' words on the subject. When asked by one of the teachers of the law which commandment was most important, Jesus answered, "Love the Lord your God with all your heart and with all your soul and with all your mind and with all your strength. . . . Love your neighbor as yourself. There is no commandment greater than these" (Mark 12:30–31).

Lest we have difficulty defining who our neighbors actually may be, Christ's words again leave no room for argument:

Love your enemies, do good to those who hate you, bless those who curse you, pray for those who mistreat you. If someone strikes you on one cheek, turn to him the other also. If someone takes your cloak, do not stop him from taking your tunic. Give to everyone who asks, and if anyone takes what belongs to you, do not demand it back. Do to others as you would have them do to you. (Luke 6:27–31)

Jesus defined authentic love for us as one in which we become fully human by developing the capacity to give of ourselves and our possessions, to share with and care for others on increasingly demanding levels of responsibility, to communicate despite our fear, and to suffer caring rather than hatred. He presented this unequivocal agenda for compassionate relationships as a guide, which we, his followers, are to faithfully obey.

At the time that I was reading *The Courage to Care,* I discovered a worn copy of C. S. Lewis' *The Four Loves* in a secondhand bookstore. Whenever I'm reading an used book, I find myself fascinated by those unknown, previous owners, who share my penchant for writing comments in the margins and underlining key words and passages in Day-Glo colors. The last owner of the Lewis book was one such kindred spirit.

Each time I picked up this copy, the well-thumbed pages would automatically fall open to reveal the same paragraph on love and selfishness, marked in brilliant orange:

To love at all is to be vulnerable. Love anything, and your heart will certainly be wrung and possibly broken. If you want to make sure of keeping it intact. . . . Wrap it carefully round with hobbies and little luxuries; avoid all entanglements; lock it up safe in the casket or coffin of your selfishness. But in that casket—safe, dark, motionless, airless—it will change. It will not be broken; it will become unbreakable, impenetrable, irredeemable.[2]

In a delicate, spidery script at odds with the flashy underlining, someone had penned the following:

To love at all is to enter the brokenness of the world and be broken. To truly love is to live redeemed. In love, we choose to suffer and face danger daily with less and less thought of self. This is how we destroy evil and come to know God and care for others.

I wish I'd have the opportunity to meet the person who wrote these wise words. In my imagination, I picture the writer to be a woman certain of the power of genuine love. She has suffered through difficult life experiences and is succeeding in her struggle to love others in the same way that a broken, yet victorious Jesus loves her. She respects, sacrifices, and gives to others with an open heart in response to the openness of God's love for her. In spite of her fear and vulnerability, she chooses to risk becoming involved with others and to gently bind herself to them in unselfish service. It is her compassionate answer to the very real power of evil.

Four decades ago, the Righteous Among the Nations of the World responded with such love. Daily, we too are challenged to increase our capacity to love God and others, to bear more and more in unselfish love, and let this love permeate our lives.

In this challenge to learn the compassionately loving aspects of courage, I remember another woman's words, ones as wise as those of my unknown margin scribbler. "Everything in life that we really accept undergoes a change," Katherine Mansfield wrote in her journal. "So suffering must become Love. This is the mystery. This is what I must do. I must pass from personal love to greater love. I must give to the whole of life what I gave to one."[3] We can do no less.

Humility

The longer I live in the crowded Southeast, the more I realize that the high-country desert of the Southwest is one of my spiritual homes. The Quaker meetinghouse remains the other. Here in my corner of eastern North Carolina, neither mountainous desert nor Quaker meetinghouse exists. I have found nothing to replace the former. One of the mainline Protestant churches in town attempts to meet my need for the latter. From the uplifting music to the liturgical ritual, I've found this new form of communal worship at the same time disturbingly different and pleasantly rewarding.

Although my spirit yearns for the contemplative silence of Quaker meeting and the profound silence of the desert, I've grown thankful for my new community of faith, circle of friends, and this place where I'm constructively engaged in the lives of those I meet daily. From the distance that time and space provide, I know, with utter certainty, that living in the desert and worshiping in silence continue to be essential for my spiritual growth. Yet, when the time comes to return to my spiritual home, I will do so equally aware of the problems such living presents.

There, I've always found it seductively easy to write out of the integrated solitude of my life without fully joining the world. While engaged in contemplation, I too often cease to become involved. At times guilty of writing more about putting faith into practice than actually doing it, I recently read, with a shock of recognition, these words of Thomas Kelly:

> The experience of Divine Presence wholly satisfies, and there are a few who, like those on the Mount of Transfiguration, want to linger there forever and never return to the valleys of men, where there are demons to be cast out. But there is more to the experience of God than that of being plucked out of the world. The fuller experience, I am sure, is of a Love which sends us out into the world.[4]

Our love of God and our fellow human beings forces us to stop lingering in the comforting and comfortable solitude of our spiritual deserts and familiar houses of worship. This love leads us away from those holy places where we encounter God and takes us to that very place where we can help other people experience the caring of God through our unselfish service to them. But to reach this place of caring and remain there faithfully, we need to develop the quality of humility in our lives.

A fourth-century desert father by the name of Alonius described humility with all the succinct wisdom of that ancient, monastic tradition when he called it "the land where God wants us to go and offer sacrifice." For him, humility was more than an attitude or feeling he experienced in the comfort of the house of the Lord. It was something he expressed in this world to the Lord's children.

For us also, humility defines the way we act as well as the way we are. Involving both being and doing, humility demands that we go willingly to that place where God leads us and, once there, we give of ourselves unselfishly. Humility requires us to listen to that still, small Voice within and respond affirmatively by making God's caring presence alive through our compassionate work in the world.

Yet we as humble people can take no credit for serving others. In learning humility, we realize that in our most compassionate moments, we have forgotten self and let God's power work in and through us to give rather than receive. In the humble land of compassionate service, we move away from the safety of our spiritual homes to return to the valleys of people, who need to experience God's caring through us.

Belonging

Belonging appears to be a strange choice to include in the requirements of courageous caring. But at second glance we see that defining whom we belong to and what belongs to us has great bearing on the quality of our caring about others.

First let's tackle the question of to whom we belong. As we transcend our fear and self-concern, we acknowledge more and more that our lives are less and less our own. We recognize that we belong to God and to God's kingdom here on earth. Replacing our fear of involvement with a selfless compassion, we find the boundaries in our lives weakening. We no longer see clear demarcations socially, geopolitically, religiously, racially, or ethnically. Acting in the belief that we all are children of God, we discover that the lines dividing and fragmenting us into hostile categories are blurring. Recognizing the wonderful diversity that does exist among us, we still count our shared membership in the family of God more important than any other marks of our separate identity.

Yet certain religious as well as political forces in America today are loath to remove the boundaries and forge bonds between themselves and those who are different from them. Denying that of God existing within each person, fundamentalist Christians are only one of several religious groups who vilify a broad range of people with beliefs and practices contrary to their own. I was shocked by the overt hatred displayed by fundamentalists toward Pope John Paul II when his 1987 visit to Columbia, South Carolina, was first announced. Equally distressing has been the fundamentalists' continued damning of and even death wishes for homosexuals, abortionists, prochoice advocates, Catholics, AIDS carriers, and liberal judges.

I have been fortunate enough to live in nearly every section of this country, with the exception of the far Northwest. In the short time I have been in the Southeast, I've become increasingly appalled by the hostile race and class relations that exist openly here. Although not limited to the South alone, this intolerance, mistrust, and dislike is augmented by an atmosphere of suspicion about those on the political left, the homeless, Communists, holders of obviously "foreign" and Jewish names, the poor, and feminists, to name a few who dare to deviate from the established conservative, white, Christian, heterosexual, middle-class norm. Admittedly only a small but vocal minority, North Carolina religious and political hate groups continue to fan the smoldering embers of this hostile distrust of others who are different.

In embracing these un-Christlike attitudes and actions, we deny that we all are God's people, belonging to the Lord. Divided by skin color, bank account size, gender, cultural and ethnic heritage, and sexual preference, we forget the larger community to which we belong, where these differences are superceded by a shared vision of life spent worshiping the Creator and treating the created with the caring of courage.

Two thousand years ago, on the cross at Golgotha, Jesus Christ reminded us, in the most extreme fashion, not to forget that we all are sisters and brothers in the family of God. Predicting his sacrificial death, Jesus earlier had told his disciples that in his Father's house there were many rooms and that the way to the Father was through him (John 14:2, 6). Following the spirit and example of Jesus leads us to the Lord's house. Imitating his compassionate caring for others becomes one more crucial step we must take along the pathway to God, whose house is home to the wide variety of human beings considered God's children. We belong to God, and in belonging, we must learn to recognize, respect, care for, and nurture all others who hold this identity in common with us.

This first aspect of belonging is an easier demand to meet than the second, which centers on the question of what belongs to us. First- and second-century Christians as well as third- and fourth-century Church fathers held similar views on ownership. Emulating Jesus, they believed his followers were to share their possessions in common. This radical rule of economic equality was to take place within and beyond the boundaries of the Christian community. Jesus' followers were to give to *all* others in need, as asked, without repayment.

These early Christians understood that individual greed forms the basis of a selfish economic policy, which ignores the plight of the less fortunate, the outcast, the unwanted and unloved members of society. Selfishness leads to gross injustice and inequality in the distribution of wealth, resources, and opportunities; it also diminishes compassion, service, and caring for those in need within the community of Christian faith and beyond.

Arising out of the evil fear of involvement, which includes the fear of having to share of self and possessions, such greed has brought to twentieth-century Americans environmental destruction, the loss of our industrial base, a crippling federal deficit, a bloated military, a power structure riddled with corruption, a cynical, apathetic public, and growing millions of homeless and hungry. Fear-generated selfishness has the power to polarize communities, pollute the earth, and destroy the planet and all life on it.

Based on the teachings and life of Jesus Christ, the early Christian model of shared belongings offers an alternative to polarization, pollution, and nuclear destruction. In its place, it puts equal access to and opportunity for adequate food, shelter, health care, work, and worship for all. Its aim is to create—not destroy—communities and to cherish—not violate—one another and the earth on which we live. Turning away from the evil our selfish fear has wrought, we are called on to return to those valleys of people in need and share with them the possessions God has placed in our hands to manage. Recognizing God as the owner both of our lives and of our belongings, we affirm this fact of belonging by sharing all that we are and have with our brothers and sisters in the family of God.

Forgiveness

We develop the courage to care about others in a Christlike manner when we learn to express the genuine love, humility, giving, and sharing that is part of becoming God's obedient servants. Yet, if we are to exercise a courageous compassion based on our shared membership in God's family, we also must learn to forgive others and admit to our own need to be forgiven.

My saving this topic of forgiveness until last was no accident. In a recent seminar I gave on caring, I noticed that the women kept steering the discussion back to forgiving and forgetting. Even though I hadn't mentioned the word "forgetting," rarely did they say "forgiving" without linking it to "forgetting." And from both the sighs and heated comments made, I'd venture to state that neither forgiving nor forgetting is something we easily accomplish.

When the seminar was over, I searched the concordance and Bible to find where these two concepts were joined. Coming up empty-handed, I looked in other reference books and finally traced this double-edged phrase back to the prolific pens of Cervantes and Shakespeare. We do find unlinked references to forgiving and to forgetting scattered throughout the Old Testament, but while the references to forgiving deal with divine forgiveness of sins and our need to forgive those who hurt us, the idea of forgetting is used almost exclusively in terms of admonishing the reader not to forget the Lord or his works.

A not-so-subtle shift in emphasis regarding these concepts occurs between the Old and the New Testament. References to forgetting drop off dramatically, while forgiveness takes on a whole new meaning. Jesus called on his followers not only to forgive others their wrongdoings but also to repay evil with good. He commanded them to love their enemies and turn the other cheek when struck. Jesus clearly stated that there is no reasonable limit to forgiving others and added, in the Parable of the Wicked Servant, that we must forgive in order to be forgiven. This same linkage between forgiving others as God has forgiven us is best known in the familiar words of the Lord's Prayer.

Yet—most radical of all—Jesus, claiming he could forgive sin, declared his ministry a call to the sinner. Bracketing his power to forgive sins with his power to heal the sick, he shocked the Jewish establishment by first giving a paralytic man his assurance that his sins were forgiven before he cured him (Mark 2:5–12).

Through Jesus, forgiveness of sins becomes a healthful restoring to life based on something we tend to overlook when we discuss forgiveness: the need for repentance. Listen to what the historian and biblical scholar Michael Grant has to say about this critical connection:

Paul was not certain that repentance had to come before forgiveness; Jewish thinkers had said it did not. But the evangelists asserted that it did, and evidently the Baptist and Jesus before them had said the same: that the sinner had to repent, had to experience total change of heart, *before* this forgiveness was granted to him, and that the difference this repentance made was overwhelming. . . . Human beings, too, must forgive their wrongdoer unreservedly the very instant he repents.[5]

Remembering the definition of repentance as a turning away from evil and a turning to Christ, we now can understand why to forgive the offender fully we must also forget about the offense committed against us. We cannot harbor unloving memories in our hearts and still experience that total change of heart called *repentance*. We each must let go of the negative feelings associated with the hurt we've received at another's hands before we can forgive him or her wholly.

Our aim is to turn our backs on the evil committed and turn toward our fellow human beings with the goodness of Christ. And in turning away from our fearful, selfish responses, we begin to make life over into an act of justice, mercy, and charity. Accepting God's forgiveness for our sins, we now want to change our responses to our fellow sinners. Breaking down the self-imposed barriers of isolation, we reach out to others with a willingness to forgive them their trespasses against us and to forget those trespasses also. It isn't enough to state, "I forgive but I can never forget." The process isn't complete until we do both. Only then can we begin to experience the healing power that is a vital part of the caring of courage.

Courageous Healers

In that same seminar on developing caring and in a subsequent one, I discovered a second common misconception, this one dealing with the basic meaning of caring. Derived from the Old High German *kara*, to care is to suffer grief or sorrow, to lament, to cry out with pain. Over the centuries, other meanings have evolved, but its primary meaning remains that of experiencing and responding to our brokenness in a broken world.

To become caring then is a courageous act that has little to do with the popularly held notion of caring as the affectionate nurturing of another person. It does have much to do with a willingness to suffer the pain caused by our unjust, unmerciful, and uncharitable behavior toward one another. Forgetting self and forgiving others, we choose to share with the powerless, the dispossessed, the have-nots, the different, and the undesirables whom Christ came to minister to with caring. Recognizing the suffering that is happening throughout the family of God on earth, we dare to follow Christ's example and experience it within our own hearts.

Once this has happened, once we have entered into others' pain and know it as our own, we are capable of binding the wounds inflicted by our selfishness. Although we are wounded and have wounded others, we can become healers. Each step we take to attain the caring of courage also binds us closer to that compassionate community of wounded healers, who work toward reconciliation, toward wholeness, and toward the establishment of God's kingdom, defined by the Christian theologian Hans Küng as "creation healed."

As the third cornerstone of courage, caring demands of us an ever-deepening commitment to heal our fellow men and women, who remain hurting and divided by the politics of power, hatred, selfishness, and greed. Fear lies at the root of our acceptance of such evil, and we can reject it only by developing the courage to care.

The mission of the prophet is to articulate the evil created by our fear and to guide us toward a shared vision of godliness inspired by courage. It is no coincidence that Jesus referred to himself most frequently as a prophet and teacher. Having a unique relationship with the Almighty and acting as God's spokesperson, he railed against those who sought to destroy God's handiwork. He also commanded his followers to walk along the path leading to the caring of courage. From unselfish service to authentic love, Jesus taught us how to accurately reflect God's image through our caring behavior toward others and our caring stewardship of the world.

Almost twenty centuries later, Jesus' life, teachings, and death continue to remind us that, imperfect as we are, we need not be broken mirrors of God in the world today. And as we journey toward wholeness, we also hear the few prophetic voices that have been raised over the centuries against selfishness spawned by evil fear. These courageous prophets challenge us to reclaim our Christian responsibility to act with the healing power of caring for all of God's creation. They demand that we learn to listen, heed, and respond in the present moment and make it Eternal.

One such prophet was the American Quaker Thomas Kelly, who died in 1941. During the forty-seven years of his life, Kelly so impressed those he met with his message of caring that he was called both "a prophet whose tongue had been touched by coals of fire" and "a great light, a wind of courage." In a lecture delivered shortly before his death, Kelly warned us that the true value of activists for the world

Does not lie merely in their outward deeds of service to suffering men, it lies in that call to all men to the practice of orienting their entire being in inward adoration about the springs of immediacy and ever fresh divine power within the secret silences of the soul.[6]

Called to care for others here and now, called to share their suffering, called to serve them unselfishly, called to love, forgive, and heal as we have been loved, forgiven, and healed, we obediently follow. In that following, we discover that we have emptied ourselves of our fear of involvement, of our selfishness, of our isolation, and of evil. What remains is obedience to God's will and courage to reflect God's caring toward all that the Holy has created. And to our surprise, we find that this call returns us to our spiritual home, found not only in the desert or the meetinghouse but also in the sacred silence of the soul.

When our caring actions are thus united with the Eternal, we are ready, at last, to meet the fourth and final challenge in developing authentic courage.

IV. THE FOURTH CHALLENGE
Moving from Divisiveness to Harmony

Turn from evil and do good;
seek peace and pursue it.

(PS. 34:14)

10. Conflict

In practicing the third cornerstone of courage, we learned that in caring for others we have to return to what Thomas Kelly called "the valleys of people." Freeing ourselves from the fear of involvement, we enter into the world's suffering and make it our own. In that transformation, we finally are capable of alleviating the pain of our brokenness with the power of God's love working through us.

Experiencing the confidence, the strength, and the caring of courage as actual forces in our lives, we know how these three qualities can help us to overcome evil and grow beyond our fear. But to attain authentic courage, we also need to move away from divisiveness toward that sacred harmony found in a life devoted to and used exclusively by God.

Inner and outward peace characterizes the courageous person's relationship with God, self, others, and even the environment. Confusion and disorder have no toeholds in such a life. As the fourth cornerstone of courage, peace defines a new reality for the Christian, a reality in which we reject the evil of conflict and divisiveness in our lives and replace it with physical, emotional, and spiritual harmony.

To travel toward this new reality requires us to strip away yet another evil fear present in our lives—the fear of our own inadequacy. Starting to live the revolutionary message of Christian conversion, we harbor a fear that we can't meet its stringent demands. The requirements of the gospel and those of the world vie for our allegiance. We are confused how to proceed and, more ominous, we are frightened to proceed since we may indeed fail.

We question whether we can effect change and become effective peaceful instruments of God. Fully aware now that we are to do God's will, we question how well we can carry out these holy demands in a world that has little use for anyone practicing the radical, pacifist teachings of Jesus Christ.

Threatened by this fear of inadequacy, we grow increasingly divided in our loyalties between the sacred and the secular. We also become disordered in our perceptions of and responses to both God and the world. If we continue along this destructive path, we will allow the evil fear of inadequacy to stop us from living Christianity to its fullest. Becoming double-minded, we may choose a fear-created life of public and private conflict over a God-centered one based on the peace of courage.

The Garden Revisited

Years ago when my sons were young, I taught my first children's Sunday school class and found it a terrifying experience. The suggested curriculum was unrealistic for this age group, and trying to keep eleven active minds and bodies constructively occupied week after week proved more daunting a task than any series of adult workshops I've ever developed.

Halfway through the year, we began working on a biblical garden and, from that point onward, my teaching and their learning dramatically improved. Like many avid gardeners, my enthusiasm for cultivating almost anything that grows borders on the fanatical. In those boys and girls, I found wonderful companions who eagerly nurtured trays of seedlings into fine, productive herbs, ornamentals, and vegetable plants. But what amazed and delighted me most about the experience was the way these children intuitively grasped the lessons of spiritual growth also being taught.

The children weren't surprised when told that the word *garden* comes from the Hebrew and means "a pleasant place;" they had already suggested "happy," "good," and "full of peace." They thought it only fitting that God had wanted

Adam and Eve to live in a garden both beautiful and bountiful. And they found nothing odd about the notion that we have never stopped striving to recreate the loveliness, abundance, and harmony of that Eden.

In spite of its mythical overtones, the garden of Eden does serve to remind us of the chasm that exists between a world of sin, fear, and evil and that place where wholeness, courage, and goodness reign supreme. Our image of Eden centers on what we, the created, can be and do when we are willing to focus solely on the Creator. The garden speaks of order and security, peace and prosperity. It also suggests to us the need for obedience and discipline, submission and responsibility.

In trying to envision the garden of Eden, we realize how accurate the English poet Matthew Arnold was when he observed that we are "always wandering between two worlds, one dead, the other powerless to be born." Incapable of returning to Eden, neither can we, by ourselves, recreate what we have lost. And so we continue wandering, divided between the violent life-denying world in which we live and a nonviolent life-affirming world we can't establish on our own.

Jesus often spoke of this life-affirming world, referring to it as the dawning kingdom of God on this earth. In fact, the imminence of the kingdom was at the very heart of his message. Jesus taught repeatedly that to enter it, we must make every possible preparation for its arrival. From the Beatitudes to the Parable of the Mustard Seed, from rebuking Martha to using the metaphor of the new wineskin, Jesus' teachings were directed toward preparing us for God's kingdom.

Jesus showed us how we can end our wandering between a dead world devoid of God and a God-centered Eden always beyond our reach. We are to abandon everything and become his followers, to wholeheartedly devote ourselves to entering his kingdom, to let go of self and join in the community of the kingdom, to remove barriers between self and neighbor in our communal pursuit of the kingdom, to love the sinner, to pray for the enemy, to respect the outcast, to forgive the debtor, and to serve the dispossessed in quest of the kingdom. Finally, we are to live in peace with God and our neighbors.

In his sermons and by the nonviolent lifestyle he adopted, Jesus taught us that conflict is contrary to God's vision and will. He charged us to recognize and renounce divisiveness and the fear that creates it, for it has the power to destroy the life-affirming union we seek with God and one another.

If we are to move from a dead world to one of life, from the desert where we first met God to the garden where the divine kingdom grows and flourishes, we need to look long and hard at how fear-generated conflict separates us from God, self, others, the gospel, and the world. To overcome our fear of inadequacy and live up to God's standards, we must discover how we can peacefully establish the kingdom of God and do God's will "on earth as it is in heaven." And there is no better place to start this discovery process than with an examination of violence.

Violence

In the turmoil of the mid-1960s, a radical American activist named H. Rap Brown declared, "Violence is necessary; it's as American as cherry pie." An outrageously catchy remark, it soon made its way into our national repertoire of truisms. The majority of Americans found it more palatable than this somber statement made a couple of years earlier by Martin Luther King, Jr.: "Nonviolence is the answer to the crucial political and moral questions of our time; the need for man to overcome oppression and violence without resorting to oppression and violence."

H. Rap Brown's remark confirmed who and what we were in a world of people debilitated by their fear of inadequacy. Unlike the Reverend King's call for nonviolence, Brown's call condoned the immoral by labeling it the norm. Appealing to our coarsest instincts, he encouraged us to accept the evil of violence as the only viable option open to us when confronted with conflict. We were freed of the responsibility to examine the sources of our conflicts. Why did we need to struggle to communicate or create a dialogue between antagonists when we could unthinkingly respond to one another with force?

H. Rap Brown was an astute observer of U.S. life. In truth, we Americans have been and still are a violent people. And our willingness to do violence is firmly rooted in individual and collective laziness. We find it infinitely easier to pursue the life-denying violence of this world than the life-affirming pacifism of Christ.

Granted, the requirements of the peacemaking message of Christ are strict. To become a loving, forgiving, nonviolent Christian among people who don't share this same spiritual vision is a lifelong task of utmost difficulty. The specter of failure continually rears its frightful head.

We look for pacifist role models and, on finding them, realize that they all have suffered ignoble defeat by worldly standards. From Peter, Stephen, and Paul in the first century to Dietrich Bonhoeffer, Mahatma Gandhi, and Martin Luther King, Jr., in the twentieth, we discover that these advocates of nonviolence didn't succeed in creating a global community of peaceful servants of God. Instead, they became victims of violence. We soon ask ourselves how we can possibly succeed where these spiritual giants have failed.

Turning our attention to public organizations does little to dim our fear that we may be inadequate peacemaking witnesses. There, we see warring factions operating openly within our churches, communities, and states. We also see the violence committed within and across religious and political boundaries in other parts of the globe. Be it the Middle East, Northern Ireland, Sri Lanka, Nicaragua, or our own hometowns, we see institutional as well as individual acts of violence as readily accessible and acceptable goals.

We feel our ability to embrace nonviolent, Christlike attitudes and actions slipping beyond our grasp. Beating swords into plowshares and spears into pruning hooks is a lovely vision but when confronted with hostility, we question how well we can deal with others in a godly manner. To borrow a Quaker phrase, we are afraid that we cannot "answer that of God" in them, opening and uplifting the evil of conflict to the divine. We fear we will remain on the level of the physical world where only force operates.

At this stage, fear of being inadequate distorts our perception so that we wrongly see pacifism as an unrealistic New Testament code of behavior applicable in some heavenly garden of Eden but certainly not on earth here and now. Although Christ clearly commands us in the present tense to follow him and become pacifists, we succumb to defeatism, accepting that peacemaking cannot be practiced successfully here in this world during our lifetimes.

In rejecting nonviolence as an unreachable goal, we are saying that we have no choice between evil and good, only between lesser and greater evils. Yet the message of Christ is that we do have a choice and that is to act as peacemakers in the world here and now, no matter the consequences. The Christian option is to overcome fear by moving our lives to the level of the spiritual world where peace, not violence, operates.

Complexity

If violence marks our fear-generated conflicts, complexity marks our lives when we doubt our ability to be an effective Christian in today's world. Rather than court the possibility of failing to live the gospel of Jesus Christ, we crowd our schedules so that we have less and less time to devote to becoming courageous disciples of Christ. Fully occupied with worthwhile activities, we hope that we need never confront the fear of our own inadequacy. But the fear that gives rise to complexity also moves us farther away from God.

The busyness of a life removed from God's influence does create an inner conflict that can't be easily quelled. And as psychologists of widely divergent persuasions have often pointed out, inner conflict produces outer conflict. Once we know God and develop the courage to believe in Christ's message for the world, we find it increasingly difficult to turn our backs on either the Almighty or the world. To grow, we must stop the internal and external struggle between the demands of following Christ and the demands that fear places on us to avoid spiritual growth and radical Christian action.

Living a complex life out of fear can be disguised in a number of subtle ways that give us little inner peace and negatively influence those who work, live, and play with us. The following questions challenge us to explore those areas in our busy lives where complexity may be masking fear and causing inner and outward conflict:

- Do I choose duties in my church that compel me to become a more responsible citizen in the kingdom of God?
- Do I seek those jobs in my community that require me to answer Christ's call to peacemaking with specific actions?
- Do the products of my working hours advance the kingdom of God here on earth?
- Do the hours I spend practicing specific spiritual disciplines give me a clearer vision of how I can best put my Christian beliefs into action?
- Do I attempt to create Christlike attitudes and practices with my choice of recreation?

Our television and reading habits, our friendships, our community and church activities, our professional choices, our worship, and our prayer life all reflect the strength or weakness of our commitment to the gospel of Jesus Christ. We may spend much of our day and late into the night in Christian activities and still allow fear to rob us of the courage we need to be true followers of Christ. And when this fear of inadequacy governs our behavior, we invite the evil of conflict to enter into all our relationships.

Rigidity

The person fearful about his or her adequacy can give expression to that fear by developing a rigid dogmatism alien to Christ's gospel. Whether we fall prey to mechanical literalism or sterile legalism, we are guilty of practicing what A. W. Tozer called "orthodoxy without the Holy Spirit." This refreshingly clear-sighted, conservative American minister understood that we in the modern Church must return to practicing godliness out of the crucible of our own personal experience of God. He refused to substitute rigid doctrines, right opinions, or "correct" interpretations of truth for his own experience of the divine. Knowing that mere words alone can't nourish the soul, he urged us to find God through personal experience. Otherwise, we would not be better off for having heard the Word of God.

I'd venture to say that we are in an age of increasing religious rigidity produced by our fear of inadequacy. Rather than deepening our private and corporate worship experiences in order to discover how best to obey God's will, we settle either for a legalistic Christianity, which renders reasonable debate impossible, or for a literalistic Christianity, which denies us the freedom that Christ provides.

In both instances, we close ourselves off from hearing God speak to us through a passage, a person, or an event in our lives. Knowing the proper exposition of a biblical text doesn't mean we know God. Nor can we know what God wants us to do without being open to the varied ways that the Almighty speaks to us.

Such openness is anathema to the frightened advocates of dogmatism, who cling to an unchanging set of rules and teachings, allowing no deviation or alternative interpretation. The rigid dogmatist forgets that Christianity is essentially a *revealed* religion, one in which God shows the divine to the human in a personal way demanding our response. God speaks to us to challenge and activate us. The Almighty doesn't so much give information as guide us in our efforts to change into the likeness of Christ. Filled with the fear of inadequacy, we avoid this need to change and become Christlike by substituting rigidity for personal communion with our Creator.

In such an environment, the evil of private and institutional conflict can flourish, for with our fear-filled behavior we are openly disobeying God's call to courage. We experience God less and less and the peace of God hardly at all. Our attitudes and actions deny the validity of Christ's statement: "My peace I give unto you." By embracing orthodoxy without the Spirit, we show how deeply our fear runs. Although Jesus seeks to fulfill his promise to us, we doubt we are able to experience that healing peace.

To feel Christ's peace within and to work effectively for peace in an evil world, we need to remove the rigid shackles that our fear of being inadequate has created. Following Jesus' call to become courageous peacemakers grows easier only when we recognize and reject all forms of conflict-producing rigidity.

Competition

Simply put, our urge to compete is created by fear, and it always causes conflict. Afraid that we can't live up to Christian standards of justice, mercy, and equality, we choose competition over cooperation and hang a deceptive mantle of respectability on our actions. Just listen to the oft-quoted words of Andrew Carnegie extolling the virtues of competition:

While the law [of competition] may be sometimes hard for the individual, it is best for the race, because it insures [sic] the survival of the fittest in every department. We accept and welcome, therefore, as conditions to which we must accommodate ourselves, great inequality of environment, the concentration of business, industrial and commercial, in the hands of a few, and the law of competition between these, as being not only beneficial, but essential for the future progress of the race.[1]

Instead of helping to usher in Christ's kingdom, competition fosters economic injustice, militarism, the threat of nuclear war, racism, sexism, environmental abuse, and other personal and corporate expressions that create conflict. Embracing competition, we become incapable of effectively proclaiming the good news, the gospel, to anyone but the wealthy, successful, and powerful.

We have abandoned those to whom Christ specifically preached. The poor and dispossessed have no voice in our competitive world. Neither do those who relate the gospel to the collective evils of our times. Succumbing to the enticing promises of wealth and power that competition offers, we ignore Jesus' command to turn away from evil and embrace good. Instead, we rewrite the gospel definition of good, making it one of earthly abundance and prosperity through the use of competition.

We refuse to see the evil that competition causes or to take responsibility for the conflicts arising from it. It is easy for us to become overwhelmed by dark visions of oppressed minorities, starving children, eroding fields, stripped forests, manipulative capitalists, secretive military officers, and lying politicians. It is also terrifyingly difficult to imagine ourselves as messengers of the gospel in such an environment. Called to obey God in all the work we do, we grow fearful of placing faith in our own work. We view as futile our efforts to change competitive attitudes and peacefully restructure the government, economy, technology, church, family, or even self.

We have misunderstood our task as Christians. We are to create the peace of courage in our lives not because we hope for world-changing results but rather to set up signs along the road, pointing toward the transformation of this world into a peaceable kingdom of God. None of our peacemaking efforts are wasted if we only recognize that through them God's work continues to be done.

Dual Citizenship

When we were removed from the garden of Eden, the Creator-created relationship radically changed. So did the harmony we experienced with other living things and the world. Since that time, we've struggled to restore our broken relationships with God and the rest of creation. Separated from the Deity, one another, and nature, we seek a return to that place where all our relationships are in harmony, starting with our central one with God.

Authentic courage is rooted in the awareness that our present as well as future centers on the kingdom of God where our relationships, both divine and human, grow toward healing and wholeness. With such courage, we find no need for cleavage between the sacred and secular, religion and life. Waiting for paradise to be born anew, we paradoxically work toward rebuilding a garden here on an earth that holds both good and evil.

Confronted by the reality of evil daily, we find comfort in a reassuring statement repeated six times in the first chapter of the first book of the Bible: "And God saw that it was good." In creating this world and all that inhabit it, God imbued all of creation with goodness and was delighted in the goodness created. We are God's, and we are good. We have a unique place in creation and a unique responsibility to it all. Citizens of both the spiritual and physical worlds, we are servants of the land, one another, and the King who reigns over both.

Holding this dual citizenship requires us to do our Lord's work in this world by creating peace and seeking justice for all of creation. There's a certain arrogance to pretending otherwise. As Jesus bluntly reminded us in the Parable of the Talents, we are to use what God has entrusted to us to fulfill the divine purpose here and now.

As an integral part of society so constructed that conflict is rampant in all our relationships, we are called by Christ to assume our share of responsibility for the causes of these conflicts and work toward ending them. In searching for the garden of Eden, we cannot lessen our concern for cultivating the one we now inhabit. If we willingly accept our dual citizenship, we must help in constructing a peaceful kingdom here while seeking beyond. And we can accomplish this most effectively by learning to fashion nonviolent tools for resolving conflict. Despite our fear of being inadequate peacemakers, we, the children of God and the children of Eve and Adam, are ready to learn how to beat our swords into plowshares and our spears into pruning hooks. The peace of courage demands that we do.

11. Nonviolent Resistance

In 1893, a twenty-four-year-old Indian lawyer innocently broke an unwritten law. Traveling by railway across the state of Natal in South Africa, he boarded the train and sat in the first-class compartment reserved for him by his employer. When the train entered the mountain town of Maritzburg, a European entered the compartment, and on seeing the dark-skinned young man sitting there, called the nearest railway official. Indians were expected to travel third class, the conductor explained to the lawyer, dismissing the ticket he clutched in his hand. Outraged, the Indian argued that he had every right to stay where he was rather than move to third class. The police were called in. The young lawyer was pushed out of the train onto the deserted, unlit platform of the railway station of Maritzburg. The railway official had taken possession of his overcoat and luggage, leaving him shivering in the night air. There he sat for the entire night, battling both the mountain cold and his turbulent emotions.

Asked much later in life what was the most creative incident he had experienced, Mohandas Gandhi told the story of this night in the Maritzburg railway station. During that long cold night, a transformation began within him, a transformation that led him along a path from fear to courage. His life of conflict was transformed into one embodying nonviolent love rooted in discipline, patience, and a readiness to suffer rather than to retaliate. Before that night in Maritzburg, the shy, uncertain Gandhi had been incapable of speaking aloud in court and had been mockingly called the "briefless barrister" by his associates. During that Maritzburg night, this same young man unlocked within himself the ability to feel and act with nonviolent love toward both the oppressed and the oppressor.

Although it would be another decade and a half before Gandhi fully developed and lived *satyagraha,* the path to true and lasting nonviolence, he took his first steps that long cold night when he made the decision never to yield to force and never to use force to win a cause. The young Gandhi rightly knew that his first opponent in nonviolent resistance wasn't the arrogant European, the callous railway official, the Natal policeman, or the South African government. He spent the first decade of transformation waging his fiercest nonviolent campaign within himself. He realized that only when he had been transformed into a true *satyagrahi* could he hope to transform other lives, a country, a subcontinent, or a world.

Before Mohandas K. Gandhi could bring about any measure of freedom for victim and aggressor alike in South Africa and, later, in India, he had to place all his relationships within the context of a nonviolent love, in which a willingness to suffer was the hallmark. As Gandhi explained, we must accept that

Nonviolence in its dynamic condition means conscious suffering. It does not mean meek submission to the will of the evil-doer, but it means pitting of one's whole soul against the will of the tyrant. Working under this law of our being, it is possible for a single individual to defy the whole might of an unjust empire to save his honor, his religion, his soul, and lay the foundation for that empire's fall or its regeneration.[1]

No ivory tower theory, nonviolent confrontation became a clearly defined way of living for this spiritual leader, rightly called Mahatma, "great soul." His nonviolent attitudes and actions did bring some degree of political freedom for Indians in colonial South Africa of the early twentieth century. Thirty years later, he also obtained freedom from foreign rule for his beloved India without violating his spiritual principles of nonviolence.

Over and over again, Gandhi reminded us that nonviolent resistance must spring from our truthful, loving relationship with God. When we are thus grounded, we are given the power to alter the fabric of our lives. Yet the practical effectiveness of nonviolence doesn't stop there. We now possess a powerful, spiritual tool for redressing grievances and righting social wrongs, a tool that banishes our fear of being ineffectual.

We learn that to end the evil of conflict, we must persuade our adversaries of the good that arises from sharing a nonviolent vision. They must grow to see that both we and they have much more to gain in harmony than in divisiveness. Converted to this vision, we hope to spark a similar conversion within our opponents. And the most effective way to accomplish that is by our loving, nonviolent thoughts and deeds.

We accept the burden of showing them how we together can become participants in the search for a creative, peaceful solution to conflict. We no longer are fearful that we will be inadequate for the task. Using trust, sympathy, and a readiness to suffer, we offer our adversaries a new vision. By fearlessly opening our hearts to our enemies, we are certain we cannot fail. As Gandhi stated in the middle of the South African nonviolence campaign of 1914,

No matter how often a *satyagrahi* is betrayed, he will repose his trust in the adversary. . . . relying as he does upon his own strength, he will not mind being betrayed by the adversary, will continue to trust in spite of frequent betrayals, and will believe that he thereby strengthens the forces of truth and brings victory nearer.[2]

Seeing one another as children of God, we seek to win over our enemies, first and foremost, with cooperation built on mutual confidence and respect. With such a basis, resolving our conflicts nonviolently becomes possible but not inevitable. As the preferred method of conflict resolution, cooperation doesn't always happen, leaving us to find a new way to change our adversaries' hearts and to reject their violent, oppressive claim upon us.

Whether we choose civil disobedience, strikes, demonstrations, marches, or other methods of noncooperation with evil, we must always strive to melt our opponents' resistance and alter their violent vision. But we cannot accomplish that by inflicting suffering on others. Rather, we must accept suffering for ourselves. With our acts of nonviolent resistance, we don't aim to coerce. We seek only to open our enemies' hearts and minds to the suffering they've created and the damage they've done to themselves as well as to others.

Our loving, peaceful, patient thoughts and actions must be directed toward those who hurt and oppose us most. In that way, we free both sides in a conflict from fear and its attendant evil. As the English historian Arnold Toynbee remarked when the Imperial British troops left India in 1947, Gandhi had not only liberated India, he had also liberated Great Britain.

Nonviolent resistance ultimately shows us the way to effectively obstruct evil without doing personal violence to its perpetrators. In following what the Quakers call "bearing witness," we first accept responsibility by becoming aware of both the evil of conflict present in our lives and our fear of battling it adequately. Next we take direct nonviolent action to resist this evil and transform this fear, believing that in peacefully bearing witness, we will receive the grace and power to live up to the radical standards of the gospel of Christ.

Balance

To bear witness through nonviolent resistance is to transmute our fear of inadequacy into the peace of courage. Yet we cannot bear witness without developing certain qualities, none more critical than maintaining the proper balance between contemplation and action in our lives. In nonviolent resistance, we constantly strive to keep ourselves in the presence of God and the world. Embarked on an inward and outward journey, we are intent on fusing the life of the spirit with that of the world.

Our goal is to have our spiritual lives become lives of action. As we live in this world and bear witness nonviolently, we continue to meditate, read, reflect, study, and pray between or during our worldly activities. It becomes increasingly important for us to set aside specific times to communicate with God beyond the perfunctory grace before meals or quiet before bedtime. Like many people, I follow an established routine before I begin working each day. Besides reading devotional material and the Bible, I spend a half hour each morning in some form of physical exercise, be it aerobics or hatha yoga. While showering, my time of silent prayer begins in earnest and continues through to when I sit at my desk. Only then do I feel ready to start writing.

Asked frequently whether I've ever been a victim of the infamous writer's block, I rather sheepishly confess that I experience it rarely. When lilting phrases in my head translate into stilted, wooden paragraphs on the page before me, I stop struggling to create and instead enter the silence in search of God. Following the advice of the medieval author of that classic guide to spiritual experience *The Cloud of Unknowing,* I've learned to summon "the cloud of forgetting" beneath which we can place our daily activities while we speak with and listen to the voice of God.

I don't offer my daily routine so much as a guide to follow as a reminder that without practicing these or other spiritual disciplines, we destroy the fragile balance that needs to exist between our inward and outer journey toward oneness with God's purpose. By helping us to unleash spiritual grace and power, disciplined reflection fuels our actions, making them less fear-filled and more effective in ending the evil of violence and hatred surrounding us.

Prudence

A disciplined inward journey empowers the outer one, subtly transforming our fear into courage. Prudence, the second quality needed to bear witness nonviolently, arises out of our contemplation whenever our self-interests are silenced. One of the four cardinal virtues in the Christian tradition, prudence is a complex quality. On the one hand, it's used to express the wisdom we show when we exercise reason, forethought, and self-control. On the other hand, it smacks of managerial shrewdness and a certain resourceful frugality. The prudent person is discreet, cautious, thrifty, and judicious.

Although prudence has been referred to as the mother of all other virtues, prudence lost favor as a popular name in the decade after the War to End All Wars. Although I'm not aware of any study that has been done on the correlation between the end of World War I and naming children Prudence, I can't help seeing a rather obvious one. Violence and prudence don't mix well together. Predicated on ignorance, violence is the antithesis of reason, forethought, or self-control. The product of evil, violence originates in greed, hatred, lies, prejudice, fear, and injustice. The violence of our first global war destroyed more than a generation of innocents. It destroyed our belief that humankind is capable of being prudent.

The first nine days of August 1945 confirmed this loss of faith in ourselves. With the advent of the nuclear age, prudence became a forgotten ideal from the past, an outmoded virtue with no relevance to the most violent threat human beings have ever created. Occasionally, a lone voice is raised in the nuclear wilderness, a prophetic one echoing the ancient call for conversion of the mind and heart. In 1973, E. F. Schumacher joined this tradition when he wrote *Small Is Beautiful: Economics as If People Mattered*. In his impassioned conclusion, he asked,

What, therefore, could be of greater importance today than the study and cultivation of prudence, which would almost inevitably lead to real understanding of the three other cardinal virtues [justice, fortitude, and temperance], all of which are indispensable for the survival of civilization?[3]

The virtue of justice relates to the truthfulness we need in practicing nonviolent resistance; fortitude relates to our ability to suffer willingly in communicating our nonviolent vision; and temperance relates to the discipline we must have if we are to bear nonviolent witness. An essential virtue, prudence binds these other three together. Only when we know truthfulness, suffering, and discipline are we capable of expressing that judicious wisdom we call prudence.

Patience

Repeatedly, Mahatma Gandhi insisted that to become nonviolent resisters of evil, we must learn patience. The patience that Gandhi spoke of is the same as that mentioned throughout the New Testament. It is the ability to endure evil, adversity, injustice, or pain with loving tolerance for those who have hurt us.

The patient person must be long-suffering and kind. Although both are laudable traits, having one without the other makes us either meek or magnanimous. Patience demands that we forge our meekness and magnanimity into a powerful force capable of transforming all our relationships into loving, nonviolent ones.

As those closest to me will readily admit, I have a great deal of difficulty being a patient person. Too often in my relationships, I show one face of patience or the other. Suffering an injustice without retaliating, I find my rising anger destroying the loving-kindness I've struggled to feel for those who were unjust. Conversely, if I have gained some measure of loving tolerance for someone who has wronged me, I find myself hesitant to submit to further suffering at his or her hands. While vacillating between the two, I become impatience personified, incapable of enduring evil with loving tolerance for the evildoer.

In reading a biography of Gandhi, I was surprised by his impatient behavior toward his wife, Kasturbai, during the early years of their marriage in South Africa. A domineering, often petulant husband at that time, Gandhi believed it was his right to impose his will on his wife. The more Kasturbai objected to his autocratic behavior, the more adamant Gandhi became. I found it ironic that the man who taught us the principles of *satyagraha* learned them from the woman he oppressed. During the early years of domestic strife, Kasturbai lived those nonviolent principles rooted in the powerful quality of patience. Her patient attitude transformed their relationship and, in the process, revealed to Gandhi that patience lies at the heart of nonviolent resistance:

I learned the lesson of nonviolence from my wife, when I tried to bend her to my will. Her determined resistance to my will, on the one hand, and her quiet submission to the suffering my stupidity involved, on the other, ultimately made me ashamed of myself and cured me of my stupidity. . . . in the end, she became my teacher of nonviolence.[4]

When patience combining kindness and long-suffering is practiced, we find our personal relationships moving away from conflict toward peace. Yet patience defines more than our human relationships. It also marks the way we relate to God. Too often when we suffer, we react as though God were the perpetrator of the injustice dealt us. We become autocratic in our demands that our suffering end. Questioning the divine purpose for our lives, we grow intolerant of a relationship in which we must lovingly persevere while God remains in control.

We want control. We don't care to wait for God's timetable to unfold. We dislike obeying Another's will that leaves us enduring adversity of one kind or another. We see nothing noble in the patience of the ancient prophets who died without seeing the fulfillment of most of their prophecies. We see even less nobility in the much-touted patience of Job, who experienced deliverance only after a great deal of senseless suffering. Yet, if we are to bear witness through nonviolent resistance, if we are to transform the fear of our inadequacy into the peace of courage, we must relinquish control and wait patiently for God. It's essential that we learn to endure adversity without giving up or trying to work something out on our own.

Speaking from experience, the impatient person disdainfully equates patience with passivity. Nothing could be further from the truth. As a central tenet of nonviolence, patience requires us to continue to be actively engaged in ending conflict and bringing about peace. We tend to forget that during those times when we exercise patience, we still are meeting God, doing God's will, and allowing a holy transformation to take place within us and beyond.

When we practice patience, the seeds of nonviolence flourish within us. We who learn patience can liken ourselves to gardeners or expectant parents. Actively involved in nurturing these seeds, we are capable of turning our patient times into productive ones, in which our nonviolence takes root and grows.

And Balance Once Again

I began this list of nonviolent qualities with balance, and I'll end it with balance, too. Except the balance I speak of now is the precarious one we must maintain between strengthening our moral standards and respecting the views and values of others. During the nineteenth and early twentieth century in the developed nations of the West, both public and private morality were clearly defined and moral standards firmly held. There was also a regretable lack of respect for anything other than traditional Western European views and values. Colonizing what we now consider Third World countries, Westerners ran roughshod over cultural or religious systems that didn't meet their own standards.

Today, the pendulum has swung in the opposite direction. Lacking a set of firmly held moral standards, we're experiencing a breakdown in public and private morality. At the same time, we've made astonishing progress in learning how to respect others. We are more willing now to see the world from another's perspective, and we actively involve ourselves in helping former colonies to develop according to their cultural and religious standards. Concern for racial and sexual equality, human rights, equal opportunity, and pluralism are routinely included on political as well as social action agendas.

We've gained this newfound respect for others at a high cost. We seem unwilling to state that right is right and wrong is wrong. Worse, we seem unable to differentiate or measure right from wrong. Yet bearing nonviolent witness requires us to recognize and condemn all the evil that our fear creates while treating the evildoer with a patient, loving respect.

We must see and measure wrong closely while teaching the wrongdoer how to respect others as we respect him or her. During this whole process, we must neither embarrass nor coerce the wrongdoer. Freeing ourselves from fear, we appeal to the wrongdoer's courage by touching the other person's heart with both our respect and our standards of nonviolence intact.

God's Singers

In the 1960s, during my first act of civil disobedience as a member of the civil rights movement, I found myself spending overnight in a Detroit city jail. Then, and in subsequent non-violent demonstrations against the Vietnam War, U.S. involvement in Nicaragua, and American indifference to the hungry and homeless, I've had to battle my fear that I was inadequate in bearing witness against the evil of conflict and injustice evident in our violent society.

Transforming my fear into a positive force for change within and beyond myself doesn't come naturally to me. I am quick to value solitude and the safety and security of my home where I'm surrounded by the creature comforts, loving family and friends, and the disciplined routine of writing. I'm equally hesitant to value the sacrifices bearing nonviolent witness demands of me. Yet here, in the midst of my comfort and security, the need to face and overcome my fear of being an inadequate Christian activist continues to tick within me. Strangely enough, the ticking isn't that of a destructive time bomb but rather that of a musical metronome. Sure and steady, it counts out the measured beats of a nonviolent song written by the divine Composer.

As with any transformation that occurs when we move from fear to building a cornerstone of courage, I'm at a loss for words to describe this mysterious process taking place within the deepest recesses of the soul. I can only say that in bearing witness we avoid compelling others at all costs, but we ourselves are compelled by this inner music of peace. Once aware of our fear, our probable inadequacy, and the stringent requirements of nonviolent resistance, we are incapable of living with our fear and the fear-generated evil of conflict and injustice surrounding us. Frightened of what Christ asks of us, we are even more frightened of remaining silent in the midst of evil. And no matter how much we try to close our ears to the transforming melody within, we find that we cannot.

The process of transmuting our fear of inadequacy into the peace of courage is in full swing, and we count ourselves among God's singers. "For what else are the servants of God than his singers, whose duty it is to lift up the hearts of men and move them?" asked St. Francis of Assisi seven centuries ago.[4]

The answer remains the same for us today. In a world crushed by conflict and injustice, our duty is clear. We are to raise our voices to lift the hearts of all who hear our song of peace. Our attempts to restore creation nonviolently may be feeble, yet the song is of divine origin, and we, like the saint from Assisi, feel joy growing steadily within us as we sing. We know we are on the right pathway, the only one leading to authentic courage and to wholeness. Having no desire to stop, we listen more closely to the peaceful melody and fearlessly repeat it aloud for the world to hear.

12. Peace

If Mohandas Gandhi was the great liberator of twentieth-century India, Rabindranath Tagore was the singer. Large, imposing, white-maned and bearded, Tagore ebulliently expressed the Indian spirit Gandhi was working to free. They were life-long friends; Tagore originally gave Gandhi the title *Mahatma*, "great soul," while Gandhi called Tagore "great sentinel." Although their approaches to spiritual growth differed sharply, they shared the same vision of a peaceful world in which the individual would be restored to wholeness.

That vision is articulated in many of Tagore's poems, none more eloquent than this plea for India to become a place

Where the mind is without fear and the head is held high;
Where knowledge is free;
Where the world has not been broken up into fragments by narrow domestic walls;
Where words come out from the depths of truth;
Where tireless striving stretches its arms toward perfection;
Where the clear stream of reason has not lost its way into the dreary desert sand of dead habit;
Where the mind is led forward by thee into ever-widening thought and action—
Into that heaven of freedom, my Father, let my country awake.[1]

Like many Westerners, I knew nothing about Rabindranath Tagore except that he was the first Asian to receive the Nobel Prize for Literature. I had no idea that any of his work had been translated into English. In fact, I didn't know how many books he had written or what type of literature he created. My ignorance ended about fifteen years ago while I was browsing in an off-campus bookstore between classes at the University of Pennsylvania. There, an exquisite, leather-bound copy of Tagore's *Gitanjali* caught my attention. In this small book of poems, I, like Gandhi, discovered a lifelong friend.

Gitanjali (Bengali for "Song Offering") is the deeply personal sharing of a man who was searching for the peace of courage. Reading his poems in this collection, I kept thinking of the famous line in Dante's *Paradiso:* "In his will we find our peace." From his poetry, novels, essays, and devotional literature to his songs, folk music, and paintings, Tagore, time and again, created and offered to God all that he was and experienced in his search for peace. Through his words, pictures, and music, Tagore became one of God's special singers, and the song he sang was an offering to do God's will as a creator of peace.

Not satisfied with these efforts, Tagore found yet another way to bring a peaceful alternative to a hostile, divided world. In the opening days of the new century, he began a school called Santiniketan, which means Abode of Peace, where he advanced the cause of world unity. Through his art and his life, the "great sentinel" strove to usher in a reign of peace where, once and for all, our terrible alienation from God, one another, and self could be healed. In place of hostility, Tagore taught harmony; in place of enmity, tranquility; and in place of divisiveness, unity.

Although his words live on in his books, Tagore's creative voice has been stilled for over forty years now. Gandhi has been silent nearly as long, his life abruptly ended by an assassin's bullet. Yet the song of peace-creating continues, sung by countless individuals in groups throughout the world dedicated to transforming the evil of conflict into peace. Although their numbers may be statistically tiny, their influence on the world is not. Be it the American Friends Service Committee, Bread for the World, Amnesty International, World Peacemakers, Witness for Peace, International Fellowship of Reconciliation, Sojourners, CROP, Stockholm International Peace Research Institute, Physicians for Social Responsibility, Oxfam, Church Women United, Greenpeace, the Friendship Force, Habitat for Humanity, Citizens Exchange Council, or Global Awareness

Through Experience, these people are raising their voices to restore creation by expressing and teaching the peace of courage.

Knowing that the kingdom of God exists within us and within this world, we are called on to create a reign of peace together based on the biblical concept of *shalom*. Here, with and through God's love and power, we can transform disorder into harmony and hatred into love. Unified in our vision, we are able to reject fear-generated divisiveness and seek the peaceful cornerstone of courage, which helps us bring a healing wholeness to all creation. But to do this effectively, we must restore our trust, our freedom, and our adequacy by learning cooperation, centering, and simplification.

Cooperation

If we are to restore God's kingdom by creating a peaceful world, we must first restore our trust in God, each other, and ourselves. And there is no better way to restore trust than by replacing competitive thoughts and actions with cooperative ones. Since I've already spoken about the evils of competition in an earlier chapter, let's take a closer look at the good that cooperative attitudes and actions can accomplish.

A Shaker story tells how one of the sisters in the Watervliet, New York, community watched one hot morning while two brothers sweated and strained over a two-man saw. With the simple practicality of this uniquely American religious sect, she didn't see the men but the problem—two people working at backbreaking labor and producing little for all their effort. Turning to God, she asked for help in finding a solution, and suddenly it came to her. She gave specifications to her Shaker brethren, they followed them exactly, and the world's first circular saw was created, a saw that not only wasted very little motion but also could be used by two people to do the work in one day required of thirty men before.

Seen as gifts from God, Shaker inventions include the felt broom, the washing machine, the screw propeller, the threshing machine, the double-chambered wood stove, water repellent cloth, labor-saving horse rakes and harrows, the chimney cap, and a folding pocket stereoscope. Anonymous, cooperative efforts all, these inventions reflect the high standards of Shaker work and Shaker honesty. They created them to both honor God and help their brethren. In doing so, they gained the trust of Shakers and non-Shakers alike, for their products were excellent and their guarantees believable.

Another group that sought to restore trust in a world sadly lacking it was the early Quakers. Referring to themselves as Publishers of Truth, they struggled together to rediscover the Divine Presence in the midst of their worship by going beyond words about God to experiencing God directly. This corporate and cooperative searching led them to listen to the inner Voice and obey it faithfully in their daily lives. In an age of violence, intolerance, and repression, they fearlessly expressed convictions stressing the need for equality, harmony, and unity among men and women of all races, nations, and creeds.

Today we live in an age that knows little about harmonious relationships springing from a mutually shared trust. We abuse one another, the land and sea, and even God with our competitive drive to dominate, achieve, and excel. We have forgotten the lessons of cooperation in which we learn to work in partnership with God to restore the kingdom here and now. One observer of the early Quakers wrote that they "grew as the Garden of the Lord." Can any of us make that same claim today?

Centering

Restoring trust is only the first step in creating a reign of peace. We must also restore our capacity to grow with a spiritual freedom that replaces the rigid dogmatism generated by our fear. Flexibility, imagination, expanded boundaries, and the joy of exploring are all facets of this freedom, but they fall woefully short of accurately describing it.

I had almost given up hope of expressing how we can create the kingdom of God by restoring our freedom. But on a recent trip to the Florida Panhandle, the solution presented itself to me. Knowing my love for pottery, friends drove me deep into the swampy woodlands to meet a potter, who lives and works in an area delightfully referred to as Sopchoppy. The ride was well worth the inconvenience of muddy trails, mosquitos, and rickety bridges. This potter's mastery of clay was breathtaking. From the functional simplicity of his cups, plates, and pots to the luminous beauty of his glazes, this young craftsperson's works were a study in freedom in the pursuit of wholeness. And that freedom arose from his ability to center, an act that precedes all others on the potter's wheel. There, he brought the clay into a spinning, balanced pivot, and through the sensitive pressure of his hands, freed it to take shape.

Centering the clay is the toughest thing to learn on the potter's wheel and, not surprisingly, the first. Only as we center the clay do we allow it to take form and live. Open yet focused, we let inspiration breathe through us to create something that has unity and wholeness. If we fear our adequacy, the clay will collapse in on itself, destroying the object we are attempting to create. Only when we strive to create with courage are we free enough to keep the clay on center and restore it to creative purpose.

So it is with our desire to create peace in this world. If we are not open yet focused on the divine, if we do not center our spirit as we center the clay, we can't know the freedom of spiritual growth. Centered, we are capable of learning freedom from both external tyranny and our inner limitations. As potter and poet M. C. Richards reminds us in her book *Centering*,

When the sense of life in the individual is *in touch with* the life-power in the universe, is turning with it, he senses himself as potentially whole. And he senses all his struggles as efforts toward that wholeness. And he senses that wholeness as implicit in every part. When we are working on the potter's wheel, we are touching the clay at only one point; and yet as the pot turns through our fingers, the whole is being affected, and we have an experience of this wholeness.[2]

In the act of centering, we are offered the experience to create a peaceful, life-affirming world. Through centering, our freedom to grow toward wholeness is restored, and we can begin the task of restoring wholeness to the kingdom of God here on earth.

Simplification

While cooperation restores trust and centering restores freedom, simplifying our lives restores our sense of adequacy. Aware that our environment is complex and our daily routine busy, we long for a simpler way of life.

In that wish lies our greatest stumbling block to simplification. We can't simplify life by removing complexity from our environment or busyness from our routine. Instead, we must simplify by meeting the multiplicity of life's demands, responsibilities, and duties while we remain focused on God.

With our eyes fixed on God's purpose for us in this world, we aren't overwhelmed by either complex demands or the energy needed to meet those demands. We've made God the basis of living, and as our Base, God directs our actions and our hearts.

We no longer face a hectic, violent world alone. With God as Director, we experience the unhurried peace of courage. We feel no more fearful double-mindedness that comes from hesitating between God and the world. With our focus solely on the divine, we live an undivided life, realizing that every action can contribute to the glory of God, and all of life can become sacramental.

Simplification brings the cleavage between the sacred and the secular to an end. Working with God, we feel adequate to the task of restoring the kingdom. With the grace of God's power, we know we can create peace within ourselves and the world, so long as we continue to focus on God's will and obediently follow wherever it may lead us. We understand, at last, the wisdom in the saying of the desert hermits: "Simply seek God, and not where God lives, for God is here, God is everywhere.''

The Desert as Garden

In the turbulent final years of the eighth century B.C., a master statesman, who always managed to get the ear of the reigning king, lived in the ancient city of Jerusalem. We don't know much about his personal life other than he married a fellow prophet, and they had two children. Yet as any reader of the Old Testament will readily admit, the great prophet Isaiah is a figure endearingly familiar to us.

Despite the gulf of twenty-eight centuries separating us, we react to Isaiah with strong personal feelings. We share his disgust with the timid king of Judah, Ahaz. We, too, shake verbal fists at the luxury and vice ruining his nation's vitality. And we cheer him when he chastises his disobedient people.

When we read the Book of Isaiah, we understand deep in our hearts why he was called the Prince of Prophets. No matter how eloquent his words, Isaiah did more than rebuke, criticize, and condemn. He also dared to predict that a remnant of God's people would be spared to continue God's work here on earth, and ultimately, a God-sent Redeemer would inaugurate a new age of peace and justice.

Again and again, when those around him embroiled themselves and their nation in conflicts generated by their fear, Isaiah alone remained calm, steadied by the sure peace of courage. He would point out their lack of trust with God, neighboring nations, and one another. He would remind them of their vows to cooperate and their need for freedom. But always he kept his eyes fixed on the Lord, who spoke to him in such a richness of ways.

As a prophet, Isaiah knew it was his duty to speak for God and interpret God's will to the godly and ungodly alike. Although his advice was rarely heeded, Isaiah continued to focus on the Lord, proclaim the Almighty's words, and denounce the evil present in Judah. Jewish tradition has it that fulfilling his duty cost the prophet his life. Tired of Isaiah's dire predictions and critical sermons, King Manasseh had him executed by being sawn in half.

Manasseh may have silenced God's spokesperson but not his vivid words. And I find few words so beautiful as those comprising what is called the restoration poetry of end times, found in the thirty-fifth chapter of the Book of Isaiah, which begins thus:

> The desert and the parched land will be glad;
> the wilderness will rejoice and blossom.
> Like the crocus, it will burst into bloom;
> it will rejoice greatly and shout for joy.
>
> (ISA. 35:1–2)

Isaiah spoke repeatedly of a time when *shalom* would reign, as in the garden of Eden. The Prince of Prophets also saw that this reign would be ushered in by the Prince of Peace, Christ. Jesus of Nazareth fulfilled Isaiah's prophecy, calling us to himself so that together we could work to restore the kingdom of God within ourselves and in this world. His life, death, and resurrection reconciled our dual citizenship in the physical and spiritual realms. He took Isaiah's vision of harmony between humanity and the rest of creation and made it a peaceful reality, which we could establish in partnership with him.

The ironic, and perhaps most overlooked, aspect of the Prince of Peace's kingdom is that it is one where the desert wilderness rejoices and blossoms, where

> Water will gush forth in the wilderness
> and streams in the desert.
> The burning sand will become a pool,
> the thirsty ground bubbling springs.
> In the haunts where jackals once lay,
> grass and reeds and papyrus will grow.
> And a highway will be there;
> it will be called the Way of Holiness.
>
> (ISA. 35:6–8)

Abandoning the desert in search for the garden, we discover that our spiritual journey hasn't led us away from the desert but back through it to its very heart. And once there, we find the Way of Holiness on which we can complete our journey toward courage, wholeness, and God.

We didn't need to go elsewhere to find either the Prince of Peace or the peaceable kingdom within and beyond. Christ and his kingdom were always present. The desert, like our fear, was undergoing transformation, and our journey, like Isaiah's prophecy, brought us back to that place, which has always been our home. A life-denying world has been transformed by the power of God into a life-affirming pathway to spiritual growth and maturity.

While I write this, three very different voices clamor for recognition in my mind and soul. And for all their apparent diversity, they sing the same song to me. The first is the warmly romantic voice of the poet Elizabeth Barrett Browning, who declared that the "earth's crammed with heaven,/And every common bush afire with God." The second voice is that of the more cynical poet W. H. Auden, who discovered for himself that "the garden is the only place there is, but you will not find it/Until you have looked for it everywhere and found nowhere that is not a desert."[3]

Of the three voices the melancholic Lord Byron's is both the most unlikely and the strongest resonating within me. In the fourth canto of his *Childe Harold's Pilgrimage,* Byron exclaimed with heartrending poignancy, "Oh! that the desert were my dwelling place." Despondent after searching for a perfection unattainable without the transformation power of God, Lord Byron failed to see that we already dwell in the desert and that it is the garden for which we searched.

We, like Byron's Childe Harold, set out on a pilgrimage in which we sought the perfect Way of Holiness leading to the four cornerstones of courage synonymous with the kingdom of God. In searching for the confidence, the strength, the caring, and the peace of courage, we found our fear being transformed into authentic courage, and evil into good. Having begun this journey in the world of the desert, we also found that the desert has become the garden where we rightly belong.

Our spiritual growth requires us to continue cultivating the desert-turned-garden within and beyond, freeing both from evil and making each bloom with courage. Changed, we are also charged with changing the world. Again and again, we will need to heed the call to courage and accept each of the four challenges to move from fear to a cornerstone of courage. Only by developing confidence, strength, caring, and peace on deeper and deeper levels of our beings will we be able to attain the courage needed to restore the kingdom within and beyond.

In the clarity of the desert/garden light, we will come to recognize courage for what it really is: evil unmasked and grace revealed. Confronting our fear, we will learn to obey God and become empowered. Answering the different, yet complementary Old and New Testament commands to "Be not afraid," we will also learn to reject the evil of meaninglessness, powerlessness, selfishness, and conflict in our lives. We no longer can accept the fear of loss and change, of pain, suffering, and death, of commitment, rejection, and inadequacy. Becoming assured, strong, caring creators of peace and justice, we now dedicate our lives to expressing the same courage that marked the life of the Restorer of the kingdom, Jesus Christ.

Last night, while traveling on business, I awoke in a strange motel room, overwhelmed by the oppressive humidity of a typical July night in the South. Slipping quietly out of bed so I wouldn't disturb my husband, I went out onto the balcony and stared through the thick haze to the dim stars beyond. In my mind's eye however, I saw the brilliant stars in the luminous desert sky of the Southwest, and I silently thanked God for our upcoming move.

Buoyed by the knowledge that we will soon return home to the desert I love so deeply, I thought of another night on another Southern balcony when fear rather than courage governed my life. I suddenly realized that, since that night, I've spent my brief years in the South unmasking the evil of fear and revealing the grace of courage.

Only when each of us actively seeks the four cornerstones of courage do we discover for ourselves how thoroughly God transforms us and the specific world in which we are called to live. Through the power of this holy transformation, we grow to know, with unshakable certainty, God's perfect love working in every aspect of our lives. Experiencing this divine love that does, indeed, cast out all fear, we, at last, gain authentic courage and are free to come home.

Notes

CHAPTER 2. HOPE

1. Thomas Merton, *Contemplative Prayer* (Garden City, NY: Doubleday, 1971), p. 72.
2. William Barclay, *The Daily Study Bible Series: The Gospel of Matthew*, Vol. 1, rev. ed. (Philadelphia: The Westminster Press, 1975), p. 87.
3. C. S. Lewis, *Till We Have Faces* (Orlando, FL: Harcourt Brace Jovanovich, 1956), p. 294.
4. Mary McDermott Shideler, *In Search of the Spirit* (New York: Ballantine Books, 1985), p. 80.
5. Saint John of the Cross, *Dark Night of the Soul*, ed. and trans. by E. Allison Peers (Garden City, NY: Doubleday, 1959), p. 33.

CHAPTER 3. ASSURANCE

1. Richard J. Foster, *Celebration of Discipline* (San Francisco: Harper & Row, 1978), p. 30.
2. Abba Cassian, *Collatio*, quoted in Thomas Merton, *Bread in the Wilderness* (Philadelphia: Fortress Press, 1986), p. 26.
3. Williamston (NC) Presbyterian Church Discipleship Program notes, Autumn 1986.
4. François Fénelon, *Fénelon's Spiritual Letters* (Augusta, ME: Christian Books Publishing House, 1982), p. 239.
5. Merton, *Contemplative Prayer*, p. 33.
6. Martin Luther, as quoted in J. I. Packer, *Knowing God* (Downers Grove, IL: InterVarsity Press, 1973), p. 78.
7. Jerry Bridges, *The Practice of Godliness* (Colorado Springs, CO: NavPress, 1983), p. 26.
8. Saint Teresa of Avila, *Interior Castle, Complete Works of Saint Teresa*, trans. and ed. by E. Allison peers (New York: Sheed & Ward, 1957), Vol. 2, p. 270.
9. Shideler, p. 194.
10. Robert L. Short, *A Time to Be Born—A Time to Die* (New York: Harper & Row, 1973), p. 98.
11. Paul Tillich, *The Courage to Be* (New Haven, CT: Yale University Press, 1952), p. 161.

CHAPTER 4. POWERLESSNESS

1. Barclay, p. 63.
2. Dietrich Bonhoeffer, *The Cost of Discipleship* (New York: Macmillan, 1963), p. 99.
3. Thomas Kelly, *A Testament of Devotion* (New York: Harper, 1941), p. 71.
4. Eknath Easwaran, *Gandhi the Man* (Petaluma, CA: Nilgiri Press, 1978), p. 97.
5. Christopher Bryant, *Jung and the Christian Way* (San Francisco: Harper & Row, 1983), p. 119.

CHAPTER 5. SURRENDER

1. Harold S. Kushner, *When Bad Things Happen to Good People* (New York: Avon Books, 1981). An earnest book based on the author's personal suffering and counseling experiences, it is written from a perspective that doesn't include Christ, making Rabbi Kushner's consolation, theories, and advice on the limited nature of God inadequate and, at times, contrary to Scripture.
2. Thomas Merton, *New Seeds of Contemplation* (New York: New Directions, 1961), pp. 192–93.
3. Katherine Mansfield, *The Journal of Katherine Mansfield,* ed. J. Middleton Murry (New York: Knopf, 1933), pp. 166–68.
4. John Bunyan, *The Pilgrim's Progress from This World to That Which Is to Come* (Philadelphia: Gebbie, h.d. on the Gebbie edition), p. 350.
5. Bryant, p. 46.

CHAPTER 6. GENTLE MIGHT

1. J. I. Packer, *Knowing God* (Downers Grove, IL: InterVarsity Press, 1973), p. 97.

CHAPTER 8. SERVICE

1. Merton, *New Seeds of Contemplation,* p. 191.

CHAPTER 9. COMPASSION

1. Jim Wallis, *The Call to Conversion: Recovering the Gospel for These Times* (San Francisco: Harper & Row, 1981), pp. 13–14.
2. C. S. Lewis, *The Four Loves* (New York: Harcourt, Brace & World, 1960), p. 169.
3. Mansfield, *The Journal of Katherine Mansfield,* p. 168.
4. Kelly, pp. 105–06.
5. Michael Grant, *Jesus: An Historian's Review of the Gospels* (New York: Scribner's, 1977), p. 50.

6. Kelly, p. 34.

CHAPTER 10. CONFLICT

1. Andrew Carnegie, "Gospel of Wealth," *North American Review*, Vol. 148 (June 1889), p. 18.

CHAPTER 11. NONVIOLENT RESISTANCE

1. Mohandas K. Gandhi as quoted by Timothy Flinders, "How Satyagraha Works," in Easwaran, *Gandhi the Man*, p. 156.
2. Gandhi, as quoted by Flinders, in Easwaran, p. 159.
3. E. F. Schumacher, *Small is Beautiful: Economics as If People Mattered* (New York: Harper Colophon Books, 1973), p. 281.
4. Gandhi, as quoted by Flinders in Easwaran, p. 169.

CHAPTER 12. PEACE

1. Rabindranath Tagore, *Gitanjali* (New York: Macmillan, 1934), Number 35, pp. 27–28.
2. M. C. Richards, *Centering: In Pottery, Poetry, and the Person* (Middletown, CT: Wesleyan University Press, 1962), p. 24.
3. W. H. Auden, *For the Time Being* (London: Faber and Faber, 1945), p. 66.

INDEX